Walking the of Sussex

David Bathurst

Photographs by David Bathurst

S.B. Publications

By the same author:

The Selsey Tram
Six Of The Best!
The Jennings Companion
Financial Penalties
Around Chichester In Old Photographs
Here's A Pretty Mess!
Magisterial Lore
The Beaten Track (republished as The Big Walks Of Great Britain and subsequently Best Walks Of The North and Best Walks Of The South)
Poetic Justice
Best Sussex Walks
Let's Take It From The Top
Walking The Disused Railways Of Sussex (republished as Walking The Disused Railways Of Sussex And Surrey)
Once More From The Top
Sussex Top Tens
Walking The Kent Coast From End To End
Walking The Riversides Of Sussex
Walking The South Coast Of England
Anyone For Tenors?
Walking The Triangulation Points Of Sussex
Walking The Disused Railways Of Kent
Walking The Sussex Border Path
Walking The County High Points Of England
Contributions to:
Introduction to *While I Remember* - autobiography of Anthony Buckeridge
The Encyclopaedia of Boys' School Stories

To Jennifer Rose

First published in 2002, updated and reprinted in 2012 by
S.B. Publications, 14 Bishopstone Road, Seaford, East Sussex BN25 2UB
Tel: 01323 893498 Email: sbpublications@tiscali.co.uk

ISBN 978-185770-3689

Designed and Typeset by EH Graphics, East Sussex (01273) 515527. Email: elizhowe515527@gmail.com

CONTENTS

Front Cover: The view across Chichester Harbour to Bosham church on a beautiful winter's afternoon

Title Page: A foretaste of things to come - steep chalk cliffs between Brighton and Peacehaven near Saltdean

Back Cover: Selsey's very own pier - the Selsey Lifeboat visitor centre

ABOUT THE AUTHOR

David Bathurst was born in 1959 and has enjoyed walking throughout his adult life. He moved to Sussex in 1988 and since then he has worked as a legal adviser to the magistrates in Chichester and subsequently in Worthing. He has written numerous books on walking in Sussex and long-distance walking in Great Britain as a whole. When not working or walking he enjoys singing, cycling and unusual fund-raising ventures. In 2004 and again in 2007 he recited the entire works of Gilbert & Sullivan from memory and in 1998 he recited all four Gospels from memory in a single day. He has appeared on the TV quizzes The Weakest Link and Eggheads. David lives near Chichester with his wife Susan and daughter Jennifer.

AUTHOR ACKNOWLEDGMENTS

I would like to thank Lindsay Woods of SB Publications for her confidence in me; Liz Howe for her splendid work in typesetting the text; and, as always, Susan and Jennifer for their love and forebearance.

INTRODUCTION

The coastline of Sussex is one of the most fascinating coastlines of any county in England and Wales. Whilst it may lack the rugged majesty of Devon, Cornwall or Pembrokeshire, it can boast quite extraordinary variety which is absent from the more majestic coastlines further west, with spectacular clifftops, wooded glens, steep gorseclad hills, historic towns, picture postcard villages, cheerful seaside resorts, harbours, dunes and marshlands with their varied plant and bird life, busy workaday ports, and of course the sea itself, at times benign and inviting, at other times formidable and angry, depending on the weather and the state of the tide. There are also the people and personalities who have become inexorably associated with the Sussex coast, from writers and composers to entrepreneurs and smugglers.

The most satisfying way of truly appreciating the beauty and variety of the Sussex coast is to follow it on foot. The purpose of this book is to describe a continuous walk along the whole of the Sussex coast, from Emsworth on the Hampshire border in the west to Broomhill Sands on the Kent border in the east. It provides a guide to the recommended route, descriptive information on the most significant features to be seen on or very near the route, and information also on public transport, accommodation and refreshment. Although it is written very much with the needs of the "end to end" Sussex coast walker in mind, there is no reason why it cannot be used by those wishing to walk much smaller sections of the coast, or indeed by the armchair traveller who simply wants an informative and readable guide to this fascinating coastline.

The book is divided into ten sections. The guide to the approved route is set out in italics and the descriptive information in Roman type, with features of particular interest highlighted in bold type. Each section also contains brief information on public transport links and a short summary of the nature of the walking contained in that section. A sketchmap is provided at the start of each section, depicting the route described in that section. The sections are mostly in the region of 12 or 13 miles long, representing a reasonable day's walking, allowing time for refreshment and exploration, and beginning and ending in places which offer a reasonable level of amenities and/or good public transport links. There is of course no magic in the sectional divisions, and you could divide your walk into longer or shorter sections.

The route is extremely easy to follow, and the directions contained in this book should prevent you going wrong at any stage. However, you should equip yourself with the pocket street atlases for West and East Sussex, regularly published by the Ordnance Survey and the Automobile Association. They are most compact, easy to carry and between them cover the whole route. Please note that the route is not waymarked and is entirely my choice. That choice is based on the need for the route to stay as close to the sea as possible without compromising safety, taking advantage of properly defined shore-side and clifftop footpaths, and avoiding too much road-bashing; in short, making a route which is interesting and enjoyable. There is no reason why you cannot vary it in places should you so wish, although you need to bear in mind considerations of safety and the danger of trespass.

The walking is on the whole very easy, and no specialist walking equipment is required. The most obvious advice is to wear something comfortable. This applies particularly to the feet: a good stout pair of walking shoes will do just as well as walking boots, and in dry summery conditions, trainers would certainly be adequate for much of the route. Nonetheless, do not underestimate the pounding your feet will take, particularly when trudging through shingle. You also need to bear the fickle English weather in mind. Unless the forecasters promise you a dry week you need to have wet weather gear with you. Moreover, gaiters or overtrousers are most useful for protecting your clothes from mud, which after a wet spell can be plentiful especially round Chichester Harbour and Pagham Harbour. Where hot sunshine is forecast - and despite the cooling winds off the sea, it can get very hot in summer - be sure to guard against sunburn, and drink plenty of water. Don't wait until you are thirsty before you do. At all times, you should also carry a supply of high-energy food and drink.

Although the walking is easy, you should be aware of safety considerations. Watch for incoming tides which can cover innocuous-looking stretches of sand surprisingly and alarmingly quickly. Stay well away from cliff edges, particularly in strong winds, and ALWAYS follow signposted diversions away from crumbling cliff faces. In very stormy weather, of which the Sussex coast has had its share in recent years, rising seas can turn even popular promenades into very dangerous places. However, providing you take basic safety precautions and avoid silly risks, you will enjoy a tremendous walk along one of the most interesting coastlines of England. Happy walking!

The Soggy Dollar is just one of the many vessels populating Thornham Marina

LOCATION OF WALKS

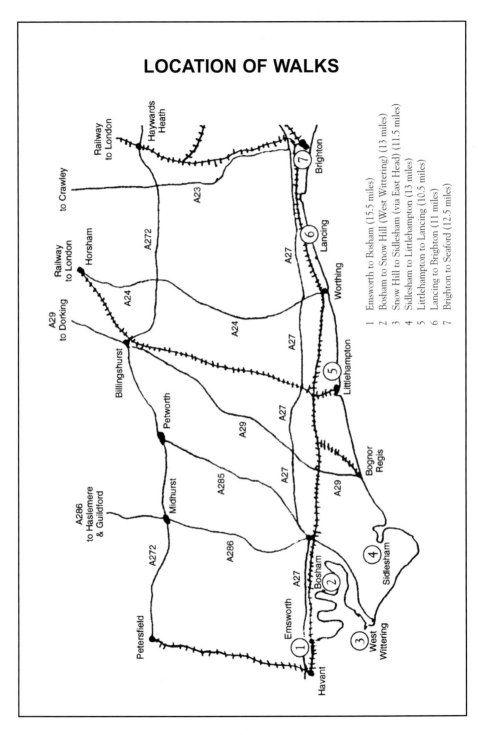

1   Emsworth to Bosham (15.5 miles)
2   Bosham to Snow Hill (West Wittering) (13 miles)
3   Snow Hill to Sidlesham (via East Head) (11.5 miles)
4   Sidlesham to Littlehampton (13 miles)
5   Littlehampton to Lancing (10.5 miles)
6   Lancing to Brighton (11 miles)
7   Brighton to Seaford (12.5 miles)

LOCATION OF WALKS

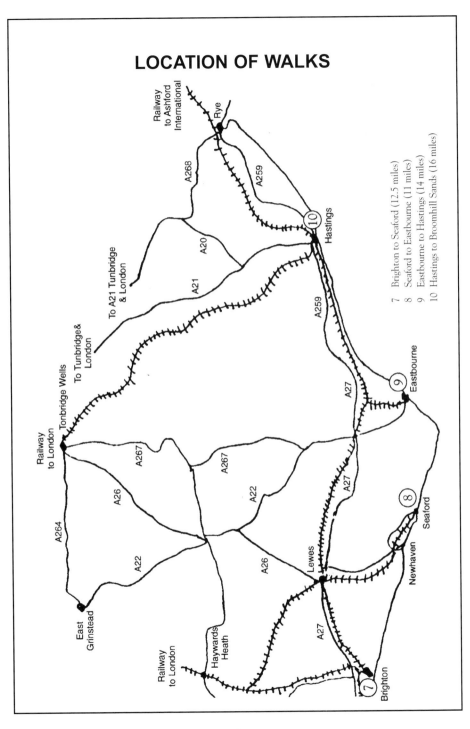

7 Brighton to Seaford (12.5 miles)
8 Seaford to Eastbourne (11 miles)
9 Eastbourne to Hastings (14 miles)
10 Hastings to Broomhill Sands (16 miles)

SECTION 1 - **EMSWORTH TO BOSHAM**

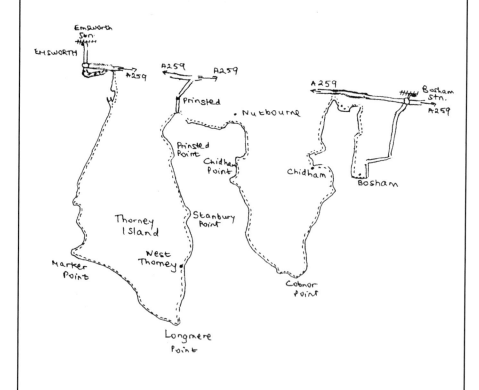

SECTION 1 - **EMSWORTH TO BOSHAM**

Length:	15.5 miles.
Start:	Emsworth station.
Finish:	Bosham (harbour end of Bosham Lane).
Public transport:	Regular trains serving both Emsworth and Bosham on the Portsmouth-Chichester-Worthing-Brighton line.
Refreshments:	Emsworth (P,C,S); Southbourne (P - off route); Chidham (P - off route); Bosham (P,C).
Conditions:	Some might say this was not coastal walking at all, as your walk takes you round Chichester Harbour, following two sizeable peninsulas with no sight or sign of open sea. However it is immensely enjoyable walking, along excellent harbourside paths virtually throughout, with superb views on a clear day and a plethora of bird life and plant life. Note however that the state of the tide will dictate the course of your final half mile and there may be some backtracking necessary which you won't appreciate at the end of a long day.

Emsworth

Emsworth, at the north-western edge of Chichester Harbour, is a most attractive place to begin your journey. Although it is in Hampshire and not therefore strictly part of the Sussex coastal walk, it provides the nearest rail terminal to the point at which the county boundary meets the shoreline. This picturesque town, which has its origins in the early 12th century, was for a long time an extremely busy and important fishing port, and by the 19th century many other trades and professions were thriving in the town. Shipbuilding and milling also thrived, with four mills in existence in or around the town during that period. It was only during the early years of the 20th century that all Emsworth's traditional industries fell into decline. Nowadays, no shipbuilding takes place at Emsworth, and the only boats that ply the waters of Chichester Harbour round Emsworth are pleasure boats. The last mill ceased to function in 1970 - although flour production had ceased there long before - and the old mills have now been converted, one of them into the headquarters of the **Slipper Sailing Club.** The little town centre still boasts a number of independent stores including a butcher and greengrocer (more than can be said for nearby Chichester!) and its autumn Food Fair has become a major and very popular local event.

Beginning from the station, you turn right onto North Street and follow it to arrive at a roundabout junction with the A259. Use the underpass on the left to join Emsworth High Street immediately beyond the roundabout, and follow the High Street to the delightful town centre. At the junction in the centre, keep to the left and continue along the High Street which becomes Queen Street and veers sharp left, passing the impressive red brick old flour mill. Descend gently to arrive at the A259 and turn right, keeping Slipper Mill Pond immediately to your right. As the name implies, the pond served Slipper Mill, constructed in 1760, and beside the pond stand the houses into which Slipper Mill was eventually converted. You see Lumley Road going away to the left, and almost immediately beyond it you turn right, away from the main road, down Slipper Road; the road soon peters out but you continue in the same direction across an area of gravel, soon arriving at Emsworth Yacht Harbour. Keep straight ahead, entering the marina complex, aiming just to the right of the black wooden sheds you can see ahead. Immediately beyond the sheds you veer left and then almost straightaway bear right(by the Deck Café) into Mill Quay. Follow Mill Quay, with its gravelled surface, keeping houses to your left; at the end, ignoring a rather strangely placed footpath sign, pass between the boats to arrive at a T-junction with a broad track. Turn right to follow it to the end, arriving at the waters of Chichester Harbour and a path junction. A footpath is signed right here, but it soon reaches a dead end (at the mouth of the yacht harbour). Accordingly, bear left to begin your walk beside Chichester Harbour, keeping it close by to your right.

Chichester Harbour

Chichester Harbour was formed after the last Ice Age by rivers of snow-melt and thawing permafrost; the gravel and stone carried by the rivers scoured out the harbour bed, and as the sea level rose, the English Channel was formed, and the harbour was created. You will follow the harbour all the way round to its south-eastern end at West Wittering, starting now as you join the waterside path. There are excellent views across the harbour to Hayling Island and the causeway linking the island with the mainland. It is hard to visualise the steady procession of malt and flour-bearing vessels which once plied these waters.

Stretching back - the coast path looking back from Thornham Marina towards Thorney Island

Initially you have a choice between a ridge-top path or a rather wider but lower one which runs parallel with it to the left. The former is more enjoyable and quite safe.

Both paths, however, arrive at a formidable looking fence, and locked gate, signifying that you have now reached Thorney Island, an important military base. To have the gate unlocked for you and progress further, you need to press the entry button and wait for the click!

Thorney Island

Thorney Island once really was an island, separated from the mainland by a channel that is marked on maps as the **Great Deep** - a dramatic-sounding name for a fairly modest strip of water. Historically, Thorney has never been a wealthy place; the lot of the landowners was made harder by the fact that over the years, the sea made significant inroads into the island. In 1870, 178 acres of land were reclaimed from the sea, and a small area of land across the Great Deep was "created," joining Thorney to the mainland to make it a peninsula. You will venture across part of that land to continue your journey. The great walker John Merrill, who made history by walking the coastline of Great Britain in 1978, still decided it was an island and missed it out of his itinerary. It is perhaps too late to accuse him of cheating!

The land reclamation was a huge turning point in Thorney's history. The population, which had been just 93 in 1861, had risen to 148 by the start of the twentieth century, although it remained a quiet agricultural community until the mid 1930's. However the Government decided, as part of defensive measures against the menace of Hitler, to install a new military air base there, with a proper access road which of course the land reclamation made possible. In 1937 the RAF moved in, and the civilian population began to leave; the school on the island had to close in 1938 as it was in the path of the new runway. The island did indeed become very vulnerable to German bombers, with a number of air attacks being made on the base in 1940, and it was necessary to install false landing lights on Nutbourne marshes further east in order to ward off further enemy activity. The RAF remained until 1976; after they left, a number of Vietnamese boat people were billeted on the island for a time, and subsequently the island became an Army base. The base is almost a village in itself with married quarters, shops, leisure facilities, medical centre, and school used mainly by the children of servicemen.

St Nicholas' Church is Thorney's most interesting building. Founded in 1100 by Bishop Warlewaste, only a small section of the original structure remains, and most of today's structure is late 12th and 13th century, with Norman windows still remaining and also a cylindrical Norman font, raised on two rude layers of stone. The church is notable for its unusual length (120ft by 20ft), and its massive tower at its western end which has reputedly been a receptacle of contraband goods. The churchyard contains the graves of soldiers and airmen of many nationalities who were killed during the World War 2. It ceased to be used as a parish church in 1981, and is now a chapel of ease used by the Army.

You now begin a pleasant and straightforward walk round the former island. It is important to keep to the path on the water's edge; do not be tempted to stray outside the line of yellow posts. At Marker Point you swing eastwards and then south-eastwards, and for the first time your walk will feel like a true coastal walk, with the sight and sound of the waves lapping the shores at high tide. The path temporarily leaves the water's edge, going round the landward side of an area of quite dense vegetation, but soon returns to the sea and reaches the south-eastern tip of Thorney at Longmere Point.

Longmere Point and Pilsey Island

Longmere Point is a fine place to pause and enjoy splendid views in all directions. Inland are the fine wooded hills around Kingley Vale, while out to sea you can admire the Manhood peninsula culminating in the great sand spit of East Head, still a good twenty-four miles ahead of you! Immediately in front of you is Pilsey Island, with its tremendous array of bird life. Indeed the whole of Chichester Harbour teems with a fine array of birds including wild swans, brent geese, shelducks, curlews, red-breasted mergansers, black-headed gulls, dunlins, sandwich terns, ringed plovers, redshanks and oystercatchers, while plants include glasswort, sea lavender and sea purslane; on Thorney itself a number of other interesting plants have been identified including horned poppy and sea holly.

The wild geese, which make such an impressive sight when a group are observed in close formation, have attracted not only birdwatchers and nature lovers. A 1799 writer recalls that "a fowler came from Dover and resided with his wife and family in a sloop anchored off Pilsea Island. He ventured out with his little boat and explored the various fowls which frequented the coast, his boat being just sufficient to contain him at full length, and in this posture he moved himself along in every direction; his instrument of destruction was 9 feet in length... it rested upon the stern of the boat, carrying a pound of shot 150 yards with certainty." It has been recorded that, on another occasion, 103 geese were killed off Thorney Island at a single shot. Some marksman....

Moving northwards now from Longmere Point, keeping to the waterside path, you pass the runway of the old airfield, one of the most significant relics of Thorney's history. As you continue northwards, keeping to a path which may be very muddy at times, you may see an Army tank being driven along the runway, and looking ahead, you will see the buildings belonging to the Army base. You now approach the principal leisure facility on Thorney, the island's Sailing Club, which is also available to civilians; at high water you must go to the landward side of the club buildings, past the church of St Nicholas. It is now a straightforward walk along a clear waterside path that takes you back out of the restricted area; one press of the button should be sufficient to unlock the gate for you! You go over the Great Deep and on to Thornham Point, once effectively on the tip of the much less extensive peninsula. You go past Prinsted Point and through the Thornham Marina, a popular base for leisure craft, then proceed to Prinsted, the village street coming down to meet the coast path. There are seats

Reassuring finger posts on the coast path on the approach to Prinsted

available for you to sit and admire the delightful views which include the spires of Bosham Church and Chichester Cathedral.

Prinsted

Prinsted is a delightful village with some of the prettiest cottages on the Sussex coast. Its name means "place of pears;" Pevsner describes the village as "incredibly leafy....the whole place is like a travel agent's poster, without any selfconsciousness....a very pleasant surprise." There is evidence of life in the area stretching back over 2000 years, with reports of a Roman pottery and coins being found in a garden in the village. The oldest and most picturesque part of the village is round the meeting of a Y of lanes, in the centre of which is a pair of thatched cottages forming a tiny square, while up the left branch of the Y stand two timber-framed cottages with overhanging upper storeys. It is possible that the materials of some of the houses may date from the 16th century. Among the loveliest houses are the thatched/timbered **Old House, No.6 The Square, The Thatch** and **Little Orchard Cottage.**

Though the village does look like a museum, traditional industries such as agriculture and market gardening have long flourished in the locality. Formerly there was a rich supply of winkles and cockles in Prinsted Bay, but these are no longer abundant, and fishing has now effectively ceased, the last working fishing boat at Prinsted having lost its registration in the 1990's. For some years there was a sailing club at Prinsted, and a large number of residents still sail locally. Arguably Prinsted's greatest "character" was William Terry, who according to local legend had a tricycle which could be adapted to travel on water and made journeys across the English Channel to France in the late 19th century. It is rumoured he was on one occasion arrested as a spy when he got there!

The coast path proceeds pleasantly on round an inlet between the Thorney and Chidham peninsulas. This is excellent walking on a firm path atop an embankment supported by very solid-looking boulders.

Nutbourne

Just over half a mile from Prinsted, shortly before you embark on the Chidham peninsula, a path leads off to the left for Nutbourne, which means "stream amidst the nut trees." In the Middle Ages there was a busy port at Nutbourne and certainly some centuries later it was recognised as a thriving agricultural community. It is recorded that there was a mill at Nutbourne as long ago as 1086, and that a tide mill was constructed here towards the end of the 17th century, standing on an embankment at the north-eastern ear of the inlet, marked on maps as Thorney Channel. It is possible to identify the remains of the hard where barges used to come up to load and unload at the mill. In 1845 the miller also called himself a coal merchant, taking coal in and sending grain products out. Towards the end of the 19th century an attempt was made at land reclamation of the marshlands hereabouts, the mill pond was drained, and the mill closed in the 1890's. Ironically the reclamation was unsuccessful, but the marshes are now designated as a local bird sanctuary and nature reserve.

A good resting-place within sight of Thornham Marina on the edge of Chichester Harbour

Beyond Nutbourne you continue along the obvious coast path and proceed down the Chidham peninsula towards Cobnor Point, enjoying good views back across to Thorney Island. Though the going is good to begin with, the embankment path soon deteriorates markedly and you may have to resort to the beach, where irregular slabs of concrete provide a surface of sorts although these can be slippery. As the coast path, having rounded Chidham Point, veers south-eastwards towards Cobnor Point, you are forced on to the shingle, and the going can be frustrating. Look left for good views of the Regency **Cobnor House.**

Chidham peninsula

The shores off the west side of the Chidham peninsula contain some of the earliest signs of human habitation that have been unearthed round the harbour, with recent excavations showing man has been here for 4000 years. Along the western shore of the peninsula flint scrapers were discovered suggesting spear shafts or kiddles (fish traps) were made here. Other Iron Age finds show that these later people had built themselves a primitive salterns, using tiny lined pits in which sea water was trapped.

With some relief you arrive at a flight of steps which take you up on to a wheelchair friendly path constructed by the Chichester Harbour Conservancy, and you pass round **Cobnor Point,** *enjoying super views across to Itchenor - tantalisingly close as the crow flies, but a long way for you! You are briefly forced away from the waterside through a grassy area on the landward side of some houses, but footpath signs lead you unerringly back to the water's edge. Good easy walking follows, with excellent views across to Bosham, until at a tiny inlet you reach Harbour Way, a metalled road. You turn left on to this road, and then right on to another road at a T-junction, but by detouring left at this T-junction you find yourself in Chidham.*

Chidham

Although the pleasant assembly of cottages and barns of Chidham is unremarkable, there are some buildings of interest, including the Tudor **Chidmere House** which fell into decay but which was restored in 1930, a well-preserved farmhouse of 1759, an imposing 18th century manor house, and the plain but attractive 13th century **Church of St Mary.** The church contains a chapel dedicated to St Cuthman, it having been suggested that his journey to Steyning, pushing his mother in a wheelbarrow, began at Chidham, and Cullimer's field on Cobnor Farm nearby was described as **St Cuthman's Field** in 1635. One well known local personality buried in Chidham is John Edes, a maltster who was responsible for commencing the building of Edes House in Chichester. The village also has a popular pub, the Old House at Home. The men of Chidham are better known for being farmers rather than fishermen or sailors, and perhaps Chidham's chief claim to fame is the discovery thereabouts of a new strain of wheat by one Farmer Woods. It came to be known as Chidham White, after its colour. Early in the 19th century, efforts at land reclamation were made between Chidham and Bosham to the east, and in 1812 an embankment wall was built between the two shores. However in 1822 a great storm flooded the reclaimed area and it was once again lost to the sea, possibly for ever.

Turning right at the T-junction, you join the road initially, but are soon able to join a path along a parallel embankment to the right of the road. The road continues northwards but the embankment path bears right to proceed alongside the shore, with the buildings of Bosham clearly visible across the creek which is known as Bosham Channel. With the demise of the Chidham - Bosham embankment path, you have to swing northwards towards the A259. The embankment becomes impossible to follow but immediately to the left there is an obvious parallel path which you join and follow all the way to the main road. Turn right to follow a pavement beside the A259 very briefly, but almost immediately bear right again just before the driveway leading to the house Snowgoose (don't follow the driveway itself) onto a rough path. It's not signed, nor is it shown on OS maps as a public right of way, but the multitude of boot prints shows how well used it is! Follow it round the side of Snowgoose and continue, keeping the water to your right, shortly climbing onto an embankment and bearing right to continue along a right-hand field edge. When your field-edge path veers sharply left it is possible to drop down (it's a steep little drop, so take care) to follow a rather muddier path closer to the water's edge, but you may prefer to stick to the field edge. In either case you arrive at a meeting with a signed path, fingers pointing left and straight on, and you continue straight on along an excellent field-edge path which veers round to the right, in a more southerly direction, heading for Bosham. This is superb walking, with great views to Bosham ahead and across the serene waters of the harbour.

Now, for the first time (and not the last) your route is at the mercy of the tides. Your trusty field-edge path comes to an end at a signed path junction (1), where you'll notice a sign saying

A golden autumn afternoon at Chichester Harbour near Prinsted

that the shoreside path may be closed by high tides. It should be clear from the surroundings if the tide is low, and in that case there'll be no problem. At other times, it may be a case of "suck it and see," accepting that some backtracking may be necessary if you've miscalculated If you're walking this section at **low tide,** it's a straightforward walk from (1) onto and then along the shore beside the creek, as it is known. There's soon the option of scrambling up onto an embankment path which takes you forward to a splendid modern red brick and flint house(2); beyond this house, continue to a really splendid house (3) which seems to protrude right out onto the shore. You could pass to its shore side, now aiming just to the left of the black weatherboarded boathouse and then walking up the ramp to the end of Shore Road by Quay Meadow, following Shore Road alongside the harbour to the bottom end of Bosham Lane(4), the end of this section, providing easy access to the centre of Bosham. Be warned, however, that the shore from (3) to the start of Shore Road is very slippery and while perfectly passable at low tide could be unpleasantly muddy in wet weather. So as an alternative, you could turn left just before the house marked (3) above along a signed footpath (just beyond the "PRIVATE HOUSE" plate) which becomes a gravelled drive; turn right at its end to arrive at Quay Meadow and simply cross Quay Meadow to pick up the end of Shore Road and follow it to the point (4) above.

If the **tide is high,** you could play safe by taking the path forking left at (1). This passes beside the back of houses, reaching a tarmac strip and then a path crossroads. Go straight over, taking care to follow the path just to the left of the gravel drive leading to Windrift, and emerge onto Moreton Road at a signed footpath junction. Go straight on along Moreton Road past the back of the Millstream Hotel, turning right onto Bosham Lane and following it down to its end and point (4) above.

Unless the tide is very high, there is a **further alternative,** which is to follow the shore from (1) above, then embankment path, as far as the red brick and flint house marked (2) above. This should all be possible outside of the times immediately around high tides. If the shore beyond the house is impassable, and at high tide it will be, you could turn left just short of the house, up a crude lane which goes forward into Windward Road. Turn right at the end into Moreton Road and then right onto Bosham Lane, following it to its end at point (4) above.

Well done - you have finished the first and one of the longest of the ten sections and deserve a good rest or night stop in the lovely village of Bosham.

Bosham

It is beyond doubt that Bosham, one of the loveliest villages on your coast walk, has roots in Roman times; not only are there Roman features in the **Church of the Holy Trinity,** with evidence showing that the church was built on the site of a Roman basilica, but it has been established that a Roman villa was constructed here during the reign of Antoninus, as well as a marble head (a portrait of one of the Claudian family), a Roman bath and a small amphitheatre. The church itself is one of the most important and oldest sites of Christian worship in the whole of Sussex. The earliest part of the present structure dates back to before the Norman Conquest with a

The view across Chichester Harbour to Bosham church on a beautiful winter's afternoon

considerable amount of early 11th century work; it boasts a Saxon tower and chancel arch, there are bases of a Roman arch still in situ beneath the chancel arch, and there is a superb Early English east window of 1120 and crypt that was built around the same time. Its most famous worshipper was King Harold, who received communion in the church before setting out from Bosham in 1064 to meet the future William the Conqueror. A fragment of the Bayeux Tapestry actually shows Harold on his way to mass at the church. Legend has it that Canute, who became king of England in 1016, lived for a time in Bosham and had a daughter who was buried in the church. After Canute's death, Bosham became the principal seat of the family of Godwin, earl of Wessex, and the lands were inherited by Harold in 1053; while the original manor house has long since gone, there does exist a **manor house** in the village, mostly 17th century, which is almost certainly on or very close to the site of the original Saxon and medieval manor houses. Although there are few surviving ancient buildings in the village, there are some houses which date back to the 17th and 18th centuries, with many attractive cottages of red brick, stone and flint. One of the more distinctive buildings in the village is **Quay Mill,** operational until the 1930's and now used as the headquarters of the Bosham Sailing Club.

Bosham used to be a thriving fishing port, with many fishermen amongst the village populace. At the beginning of the twentieth century it was second only to Whitstable in the oyster trade, although as a port it tended to be dwarfed by Emsworth. The fishermens' cottages bore such august names as Bosham Castle and Bosham Abbey! Another formerly thriving industry in Bosham was shipbuilding. Sailing now comprises virtually all of the maritime activity at Bosham and indeed the village now feeds very largely off the tourist industry with its tearooms, craft shops and galleries to entice visitors at all times of the year.

Although Bosham is regarded as a waterside village, the creek beside which it stands, set well back from the sea and effectively an inlet of Chichester Harbour, is tidal. Normally the water covers the creek twice a day at high tide, but at low tide the waters disappear altogether. When the waters do rise, the effect can be considerable, especially when high spring tides are combined with heavy rainfall; it is hardly surprising that some cottages have raised steps to enable access in times of flooding, and a raised walkway known as the Trippit has been constructed along the roadside near the water's edge, said to have been built from stones that came into Bosham as ships' ballast. Those most likely to be caught unawares by rising tides are likely to be visiting motorists; one resident of Bosham known to me recalls being asked by a lady if she could help her find her car, and my friend sadly had to point out that she could just see the roof protruding out of the high tide on Shore Road.

SECTION 2 - **BOSHAM TO SNOW HILL (WEST WITTERING)**

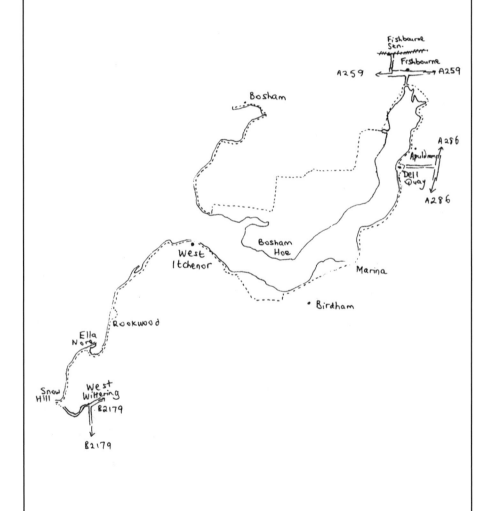

SECTION 2 - **BOSHAM TO SNOW HILL (WEST WITTERING)**

Length:	13 miles.
Start:	Bosham (harbour end of Shore Road).
Finish:	Snow Hill (easy walk to West Wittering).
Public Transport:	Regular buses to Chichester from West Wittering.
Refreshments:	Fishbourne (P,C); Dell Quay (P); Itchenor (P); West Wittering (P,C,S).
Conditions:	This is a continuation of your pilgrimage beside Chichester Harbour and after some inland road tramping in the first few miles, there is some fantastic walking to enjoy, particularly between Dell Quay and Itchenor. Note that exceptionally a combination of very wet weather and high spring tides may submerge the path on the approach to Fishbourne. There is another shorter section described below where a detour may be needed when the tide is high. For this reason, the first 4 miles of this section are best undertaken outside high tide.

With some reluctance you leave Bosham, continuing along the water's edge either using the raised walkway or Shore Road, depending on the tide. At low tide you may then use a causeway to take a short cut to continue your waterside walk, but at high tide it is necessary for you to execute a giant U turn, keeping to Shore Road which goes right round the edge of the inlet. Ignore the left turn off down Stumps Lane at the inlet's south-east corner. Now heading along Shore Road in a south-westerly direction, you pass a number of large houses, enjoying superb views across the water to the village you have just left. At exceptionally high tides this road too is liable to flooding. In due course you pass a house with a magnificent fir tree on the front lawn. Here the road bends sharply left and arrives at an area of trees, leaving the shore. At this point, look out for a footpath sign pointing you right off the road and on to a footpath that continues close to the shore. The path can be quite muddy and slippery, and at very high tides, when it is liable to flooding, you may have to stick to the road.

Enjoying fine views across the waters off Cobnor Point on the right, you swing from south-westwards to south-eastwards, and now look across the water to Itchenor, and the terminal for the Itchenor ferry. Here you turn sharp left, away from the shore, along an obvious path that takes you back to the road. You turn right on to the road and follow it - it is now called Smugglers Lane - for about a mile, your views to the harbour restricted by residential development.

At the end of Smugglers Lane there is a T-junction where you have to turn left on to Hoe Lane, away from the harbour, for between you and the waterside now is the exclusive and very private housing development known as Bosham Hoe. You follow Hoe Lane for roughly half a mile then turn right into Old Park Lane. You follow this road which initially is fairly straight then bends sharply left and passes to the right of a pond. Shortly you reach Church Farm, and a T-junction. Old Park Lane bears left, and at high tide, when the harbour-side path this side of Fishbourne can exceptionally flood in very wet weather (check tide tables before setting out!), you are advised to continue along it into Fishbourne. The coast route, however, bears right along the metalled lane which after half a mile comes to an end at Hook Farm. At the end of the lane you turn left on to a footpath which climbs gently, giving you a lovely view across the harbour to Dell Quay, and, beyond that, Chichester Cathedral. After following the footpath for about a quarter of a mile, you cross a stream and turn right immediately beyond it on to a signposted footpath which runs parallel with the stream towards the harbour. You follow the path which swings left to proceed alongside the harbour towards Fishbourne.

It is good to be reunited with the harbour, and this is a delightful walk with excellent views both to the communities of Fishbourne and Chichester and also the beautiful countryside beyond. Though the going can be very muddy in places, it improves as you join a raised embankment, and progress is swift and satisfying. You drop down again as you approach the houses of Fishbourne, and the last few hundred yards to the village are through marshy terrain which as stated above may possibly flood at high tide. In due course you arrive at the bottom of Mill Lane, with a delightful pond on your left. (Using the high tide Old Park Lane alternative, you will arrive at the A259. Turn right on to it and then, in half a mile, right into and along Mill Lane.) Simply detour up Mill Lane if you wish to visit Fishbourne.

Fishbourne

Shown in the Domesday Book as Fisebourne, it is named after the fish found in the nearby harbour, and is of course best known for its Roman associations. The invading

The well-defined coast path between Fishbourne and Dell Quay

Romans regarded the Chichester Harbour area, previously occupied by a pro-Roman tribe known as the Atrebates, as an ideal base for further conquest, and they acquired a landing place at the head of Fishbourne Channel. In 1960 workmen cutting a trench for a water main came across a mass of ancient rubble which turned out to be the remains of a substantial **Roman palace,** its interior fashioned by skilled Italian craftsmen, containing magnificent mosaic floors. It was remodelled in the 2nd century AD, but had virtually disappeared by the time of the Saxon invasion in the 5th century AD. Though the most impressive mosaic flooring in the palace, incorporating floral motifs, dolphins, fish and vases, is now housed in Chichester District Museum, a superb covered display of the palace remains can now be seen just to the north of the village centre, off Salthill Road; to get there, follow Mill Lane to the A259, turn left on to the A259 and shortly right into Salthill Road. Architecturally there is little else of interest; the village boasts a 17th century plain brick **Manor House,** while the **Church of St Peter and St Mary** to the east was almost all built in 1821, the north transept being added in 1973, and there is little left of the original 13th century structure save for a lancet window in the chancel. Nowadays the village has become a virtual suburb of Chichester.

You press straight on eastwards, in the shade of trees, keeping a narrow channel to your left. You emerge from the trees and pass a helpful information board provided by the Chichester Harbour Conservancy. You then arrive at a junction of footpaths; do not continue eastwards over the footbridge but bear right along what is a good path and strike out in a more southerly direction along an obvious if rather juicy path, now following alongside the east shore of the harbour and heading for Dell Quay. In due course you climb up on to an embankment, giving the perfect platform for views across the water. This is lovely walking; particularly entrancing is the view to the north, where you can contrast the harbour and the flat marshlands with the rolling hills behind. In due course you cross over the river Lavant at the point where it flows into the harbour. Shortly beyond the Lavant crossing, you pass two paths in quick succession leading off to the left. The second one provides a possible detour to the pretty village of Appledram or Apuldram; you may see either spellings on maps or signposts, the latter being an earlier spelling. Shortly beyond the Appledram turning you arrive at Dell Quay. Look out for a charming thatched cottage on your left just before you reach the hard.

Appledram & Dell Quay

Until the 17th century, Appledram had its own port on the harbour, and in the 18th century it had its own salterns, built by lames Ayles to extract salt by evaporation. Nowadays the village is a tranquil place. Its Early English **Church of St Mary** is mostly 12th and 13th century; features of interest include a scratch dial, the shadows on which fall at times when medieval church services might have been said to occur, and an organ which was originally made for Prince Albert around 1845 and found its way to Appledram via Windsor and Littlehampton. The finest building in Appledram is **Rymans,** a stone-built manor house named after one William Ryman. The tower, believed to have been built by Ryman, dates back to 1410; the distinctive pyramidal cap on top of the tower dates from the 17th century. Appledram has latterly been better known for its lovely **Gardens.**

Dell Quay used to be a very busy port, and in the 8th century it was ranked as the seventh most important town in Sussex. It was in the early 13th century that it emerged as the port for Chichester, and by Elizabethan times it was a busy place, with 3 vessels sailing from here to fight the Armada. Despite the activity, there were complaints about the lack of facilities such as storehouses and boarding houses, and silting of the harbour prevented larger vessels using the port. Its prosperity was assured, however, in the 17th century, firstly by the disappearance of the port at Appledram and secondly a charter of 1681 whereby Dell Quay was to be the only port in Chichester Harbour permitted to land or discharge any goods for the city of Chichester. Throughout the 18th century there was a flourishing trade in grain, and other cargoes would include bacon, butter, cheese, salt, fish, oysters, canvas, leather, lead, iron, timber and stone. A fleet of fishing boats also operated from the port. There was a mill at Dell Quay, built by William Tipper in the late 18th century. It was never very efficient and as the 19th century wore on, the grain trade began to leave Chichester Harbour.

By the early part of the 20th century, the port had fallen into terminal decline. However, the port found a new prosperity in the form of sailing and boating. A sailing

club was established in 1925, and huge numbers of sailing enthusiasts now come here to enjoy both the sport and no doubt the apres-sail refreshment at the **Crown and Anchor pub,** said to be at least 400 years old. It is reported that on one infamous occasion there was a fight between revenue men and smugglers - of which there were many in this area - in the cellars of the inn, resulting in the murder of five of the law enforcers. Incredibly, the leader of the "free traders" was said to be the local vicar.

The Crown & Anchor at Dell Quay, a justifiably popular refreshment spot for walkers and sailors alike

Arriving at Dell Quay, you reach the end (or beginning) of Dell Quay Road, the lane linking the quayside with the A286 Chichester-Witterings road. You turn left on to the lane and follow it past the Crown and Anchor and a number of smart residences. Watch out for Apuldram Cottage which you soon see on your right-hand side. Immediately beyond this cottage you turn right on to a permissive footpath which is not actually shown on any of the current maps. This path follows a field edge and soon reunites you with the waterside, and although it can be very wet and muddy after heavy rain, the scenery is superb with good views back to Dell Quay and Chichester Cathedral. You cross a small wooden bridge and proceed along a narrow dirt track, which again can be somewhat moist in rainy conditions, through a small patch of woodland known as Salterns Copse. This is still lovely walking, with the water's edge so close by to your right. You soon reach a T-junction of paths; turn right here, and go forward across an area of gravel, passing a toilet block on your left hand side and picking up a good concrete path that takes you to the lock gates. To your left is the massive Chichester Yacht Basin, with its marina and huge array of luxury craft. Providing lights are not flashing to warn you of the imminent parting of the gates to let a boat into or out of the basin, cross straight over the lock gates and continue, soon bearing right to follow the approach road to Chichester Yacht Club. As you approach the clubhouse, bear left onto the club car park and walk on through it, passing to the left of the clubhouse and shortly arriving at another set of lock gates. This is Salterns Lock, and the channel you are about to cross here is actually Chichester Canal.

Chichester Canal

The canal was part of the Portsmouth & Arundel Canal which opened in 1823 and provided a linkage with other waterways to form a complete Portsmouth-London waterway route. The section between Salterns Lock and the city of Chichester was designed to accommodate vessels up to 85 ft long and 100 tons in weight. It shut in 1906.

Between here and Itchenor, the going is more fiddly with only limited walking by the side of the harbour. Cross the lock gates and continue along the path, ignoring a right path fork by some modern houses, but then you are forced to bear sharp right along a path that leads you to a road. Join this road, heading south-westwards, and shortly arrive at Birdham Pool, crossing over the pool along the causeway. Continue briefly along the road beyond Birdham Pool, the pool of the former tidal mill(see below). The lane rises slightly and bends left, and just beyond the left bend bear right onto a signed path, in fact a metalled drive signed Harbour Meadow. However by remaining on the road you will reach the village of Birdham

Birdham

Birdham, taking its name from the "presence of birds," and originally known as Bridham or Brideham, has a long history of agriculture and fishing, with three fishing boats recorded as being based in Birdham in 1817. It was near Birdham that the painter J.M.W. Turner discovered the beauty of Chichester Harbour, and his painting of it is on view in Petworth House. Although it has become quite a sprawling village with considerable amounts of modern development, Birdham has boasted two buildings of particular interest down the ages. One is the tide mill, dating back to 1767. The mill remained operational until as recently as 1935, after which time the mill buildings, including the mill house of 1780, were taken over by the Birdham Yacht Club. Meanwhile the part of Birdham Pool on the harbour side of the Causeway became a marina in 1937, and one of the earliest marinas in the country. The other building of interest is the Church of St James which was built in the 14th century. The original 14th century chancel arch remains, as does the tower which dates back to 1545.

Two beautiful views of Chichester Harbour between Dell Quay and Birdham

You follow the metalled road towards Harbour Meadow but shortly a footpath forks left off this road; and you take this path which goes along the right hand edge of a large field. You skirt a small area of woodland that lies to your right, and arrive back at the water's edge at Westlands, following a narrow path between large houses to your left and the harbour to your right. Having passed Westlands Pier the path swings abruptly away from the waterfront and goes up to meet a metalled drive. You turn right on to the drive, passing between further large properties, and following the drive round to the left to arrive at a T-junction. You turn right and follow a metalled lane, set some way back from the waterfront, and after about a quarter of a mile reach the buildings of Westlands Farm. Just short of these buildings, however, a signpost directs you along a footpath which passes round the left hand side of the farm. Once round the farm, you reach a junction of paths; do not continue along the left hand edge of the field in front of you but follow the footpath that bears right, going diagonally across the field and then passing through Westlands Copse. Shortly you arrive at a metalled drive, Spinney Lane. Turn left on

to it and then in a few hundred yards bear right off it, following a marked footpath which brings you back to the waterfront. It is then a lovely waterside walk to Itchenor which you reach in about a quarter of a mile. Immediately before the Itchenor Sailing Club building, swing left and make your way up the path to Itchenor's village street, arriving opposite the comparatively new Ship Inn where you may feel you deserve a drink! Turn right to follow the street down to the waterfront again.

The exit from Chichester Marina onto Chichester Harbour

Itchenor

The correct name for Itchenor is actually West Itchenor. The village of East Itchenor, lying between West Itchenor and Birdham, has disappeared; it is suggested that it was destroyed by fire to prevent the spread of the Great Plague. The village's name is derived from the Saxon Icca who settled his people in the harbour after the collapse of Roman Britain, although at the time of Domesday it was a sparsely-populated hamlet. Its oldest surviving building is the Early English **Church of St Nicholas,** dating from the 13th century and retaining its octagonal 13th century font. Other buildings of architectural interest in the village include the **Old Rectory** which is a small timber framed building dating from the 15th century, **Emmets** with its 18th century walls and tiled roof, the **Sailing Club House** which is probably late 17th century, and **Itchenor House,** built for the 3rd Duke of Richmond in 1787. He had a schooner called the Goodwood which he moored here, and the house was built as a yachting lodge. The street leading down to the waterfront contains many pleasant old houses and cottages.

The view across Chichester Harbour from Itchenor

Itchenor is historically best known for its association with shipbuilding. Small warships had been built here in Tudor times, but the heyday of shipbuilding at Itchenor was in the 18th and early 19th centuries, when a number of naval ships were launched from here. Although shipbuilding at Itchenor subsequently declined, Haines Boatyard was established in 1912 and continues to this day, specialising in the construction and repair of leisure craft, particularly glass-fibre moulded hulls. For many years George Haines was synonymous with boats and boating at Itchenor. He became responsible for the ferry service between Itchenor and Bosham, which was not always reliable; often the motor would break down halfway across and the boatman would be constrained to row the rest of the way. During the Second World War Itchenor's priorities had to change, and a number of small fast vessels and landing craft were built here for the Normandy invasion. After the war, however, the village once again returned to the production of pleasure craft, including fast motor cruisers. The village has served not only as the customs clearance port for the harbour but as the home of the local marine police and Chichester Harbour Conservancy. It is now, like Dell Quay nearby, immensely popular with the sailing fraternity.

There is a coast path all the way to West Wittering, although it can get very muddy. Immediately beyond the Harbour Conservancy office near the waterfront, bear left and follow the signed footpath which soon passes a large boatyard and a small industrial estate, and then heads out into open country. You soon pass an area of saltmarsh known as Chalkdock Marsh, then proceed through a delightful area of woodland, emerging to enjoy quite magnificent views across to Cobnor Point, Thorney Island, Pilsey Island and Hayling Island. On this section you can also identify the spires of Chichester Cathedral and Bosham Church. As Thorney Island and Pilsey Island get closer, the water is now noticeably choppier - a sign that you are moving closer to the open sea.

Just under 2 miles from Itchenor your path turns sharply inland, passing between two large houses, to arrive at a metalled drive. You turn right on to it and follow it past other sizeable properties, then immediately before Bricket Cottage, the house name clearly marked on the gate, you turn right again to join a footpath which you follow to return to the water's edge. As you resume your walk beside the water, look immediately left at the fine red brick Rookwood House, with its immaculate lawns and a setting which could hardly be more idyllic. It is now a delightful walk by the water's edge on a clear path. In just over a quarter of a mile from Rookwood House you reach another small grouping of buildings, and just beyond a distinctive black wooden building, you turn sharp left to find yourself at the end of Ellanore Lane. Do not follow the lane, but turn immediately right through a gate and on to a good path that brings you to within shouting distance of Ella Nore, a spit of land that provides a fragile habitat for wildlife and plant life, including sea kale, sea campion and yellow-horned poppy.

You now enjoy a delightful and straightforward walk along the waterside, with the great spit of East Head becoming more and more prominent ahead of you. At this point you are well to the south of Thorney Island and it is now Hayling Island that you can see across the harbour, while to your left are the buildings of West Wittering. In just over half a mile from the seat and information board at Ella Nore you reach a green and the area of the harbourside known as Snow Hill. The name is somewhat ironic because there are no hills around here at all, and lying snow hereabouts is a very rare occurrence indeed. The coast route continues over the green by the waterside, swinging in a more south-westerly direction, but by following the left-hand edge of the green to its far corner you will be able to pick up Coastguard Lane and it is then a short walk into West Wittering. Buses to Chichester are available from the village centre.

Snow Hill and West Wittering

The area known now as Snow Hill was once a port and a base for fishing, with ten fishing vessels based here in 1817. Nearby West Wittering is one of the earlier settlements in the harbour area, and indeed it is possible that the Romans had a coastal defence here. In 683 when Wilfred came, the area was known as the Withtrynges or Wihthringes, and apparently a church was established here as early as 740. Agriculture has traditionally been very important to the village, and in the early years of the 20th century, West Wittering was still an agricultural parish. In modern times, however, tourism and leisure have predominated. Besides being a popular resort, the village has also become a popular place for those in retirement or simply seeking a quieter pace of life; one of its more distinguished residents was Henry Royce, of Rolls Royce fame, who came here in 1917 having left Derby in 1912, and stayed at West Wittering until his death in 1933. It was at his house here, Elmstead, that the famous Rolls Royce engine was discussed and planned.

The most interesting building in the village is the fine **Church of St Peter,** the building of which has been credited to St Richard of Chichester. The north nave wall is 11th century, and there is a 13th century chancel, south chapel and coffin lid. The church has one other interesting rarity, namely the tomb of a so-called boy bishop. Boy bishops were choristers who in the Middle Ages were chosen as mock bishops for three weeks or so before Christmas, each fully robed and treated as though they were real bishops. Arthur Cooke, while very taken with the church, reports rather less than enthusiastically of the dull drone of the bees' nest in the roof, although even that, he said, sounded musical in comparison with the sounds that emitted from the organ.

SECTION 3 - **SNOW HILL TO SIDLESHAM (VIA EAST HEAD)**

SECTION 3 - **SNOW HILL TO SIDLESHAM (VIA EAST HEAD)**

Length:	11.5 miles.
Start:	Snow Hill.
Finish:	Mill Lane, Sidlesham.
Public Transport:	Regular buses serving East Wittering on the Chichester-Witterings route; regular buses serving Selsey and Sidlesham from Chichester.
Refreshments:	East Wittering (P,C,S); Selsey (P,C,S); Sidlesham (P,S).
Conditions:	There is some great walking here with your first sight of the open sea, but some of the walking, particularly either side of East Wittering, is quite tough, with a fair bit of shingle tramping. The views, however, are magnificent and the variety of landscapes and seascapes is breathtaking.

Having followed the green along the water's edge at Snow Hill you continue to a small inlet and then along an excellent waterside path - note the crab pool to your left hereabouts, a popular haunt for youngsters - and forward to the "neck" of the great spit of East Head. As you arrive at this point you cannot miss a wide and popular path leading away to the right along the right-hand side of the spit. If you are pushed for time, you could cut the tour of East Head out altogether, and simply cross over the path and mount the shingle bank, turning left to continue. If you do decide to inspect East Head, by all means take the path along the right hand side of the spit, but the extent to which you will be able to venture out to the very top end will depend on the tide and your patience, as you forge your own path through the soft sands. You may wish to try and follow the shore right round (but be very aware of the state of the tide), or you may be content to take a short cut across the sands to pick up a path which runs down the west edge of the spit. A

The far end of East Head; the stand of Goodwood Racecourse can just be made out on the horizon!

board-walk, opened in 1992, provides a user-friendly short cut between the two "proper" paths, but the choice of route is yours.

East Head

East Head is a huge spit of sand, which like Ella Nore has been formed and shaped by the surrounding seas. As recently as the 18th century, the spit pointed south-westwards out into the Solent, and the entrance into Chichester Harbour from the Solent was as little as 300 yards wide. In 1966 the spit was taken over by the National Trust, and it remains an important area for certain birds and plants. Feathered visitors include the lapwing, snipe and black-tailed godwit, whilst amongst the dunes you will find lynne grass, marram grass and glasswort. On a clear day, the views from the top end of the spit are extraordinary; you will see as far afield as the Trundle, well to the north of Chichester, to Butser Hill, on the South Downs near Petersfield, and the Isle of Wight.

Leaving East Head behind, you now proceed south-eastwards along a clear path on the bank, with a large car park to your left. This is a crucial stage of the walk, for you have now bidden farewell to Chichester Harbour and for the first time on your walk you have the open sea to your right. You pass a long succession of beach huts on your left, but the view to your right is

Cakeham Tower, an invaluable landmark for seamen since its construction in the 16th century

infinitely more pleasing, with the golden sands and the seas, stretching out seemingly towards infinity - or, if you crane your head further to your right, the Isle of Wight at any rate. This section is better walked in the winter months, as the crowds can be massive during summer weekends.

Once you have passed the car park entrance which lies to the left, the path becomes a delightful green carpet and there are now clear views ahead to Selsey Bill, while large residential properties line the left hand side of your route. When the houses relent, look to the left to get a clear view of Cakeham Tower. Shortly beyond Cakeham Tower you arrive at the outskirts of East Wittering; the green carpet gives way to a stonier surface and, for a short while, shingle, offering a foretaste of hard work to come. The path turns left and almost immediately right, and continues past the backs of houses which look frighteningly susceptible to the elements. More patches of shingle make this quite a tough walk, but the shingle eases as you approach a large block of red brick flats adjacent to a refreshment hut. Immediately beyond this lies the road that leads into the centre of East Wittering. To continue the coast walk you turn left on to the road then immediately right on to Tamarisk Walk, but many walkers will wish to seek refreshment in the village, which is a few minutes' walk up the road.

East Wittering

Cakeham Tower is perhaps East Wittering's most interesting building. This very distinctive hexagonal red-brick structure, a useful navigation point for seamen, was built by Bishop Sherburne in the 16th century; nearby once stood Cakeham Manor, an occasional bishops' residence, and an attractive conglomeration of medieval, Tudor and Georgian, although only a few remains survive. There is little else in the village to see. There was once a

A delightful green carpet provides easy walking between East Head and East Wittering

tower mill here, supported on oak ties and beams, that was built in 1810; it worked for 80 years or so but the sweeps were removed at the end of the 19th century. Following a fire in 1975, only the brick-built middle section remains, and this can be seen in the village centre. Pevsner describes the village as "untidy," while Philips County Guide, somewhat tongue-in-cheek one suggests, writes of the village offering "fast food and other delights for day visitors."

To continue your walk, follow Tamarisk Walk beside houses. It's lovely walking across a green, but the green ends at a fence with beach huts immediately beyond, and you're faced with a rather contradictory message: a signboard saying PRIVATE PROPERTY but an adjacent gate with an arrow sign inviting you proceed along the shingle past the huts! I infer that the Private sign refers to the beach huts and their immediate surrounds, and certainly when I walked this section there were other walkers on the shingle beside the beach huts. (If you are genuinely concerned, turn left just before the huts up a path going forward into Shingle Walk; turn right at the end into Charlmead [not hard right into Coney Six], following Charlmead to a T-junction and turn right again to return to the shore beyond the beach huts.) Continue along the shingle beyond the huts; it's quite tough going for a few hundred yards, and it's a relief to reach a concrete area just to your left, which signifies your arrival at Bracklesham. There's a refreshment area a short distance away and if you need to top up your supplies, you can see a general store a little way up the road

Bracklesham

Bracklesham is, regrettably, of even less interest architecturally than East Wittering, although it has a pub called the Lively Lady that was named after the vessel in which Alec Rose sailed round the world single handed in 1960. Records show that at one time, certainly before the 16th century, Bracklesham was an independent parish with its own chapel, but the site has long since become submerged. In 1588 the Spanish frigate Cartagena was grounded in the bay and legend has it that some of her timbers were abstracted for use in building a farmhouse some distance inland, but there is conflicting evidence on the point! The **shore of Bracklesham Bay** is, however, of greater interest, for it is renowned for its fossils which have been found here in large numbers. Here have been discovered the fossilised remains of turtles, crocodiles, sea snakes and large sharks, dating back upwards of 40 million years.

Beyond Bracklesham, shingle is the order of the day all the way down to West Sands Caravan Park at Selsey. To begin with, progress is laborious, but at low tide it may be possible to seek out a firmer and sandier course along the beach. There is still housing to your left, and you should look out for a house of very modern design with its steeply sloping roof and huge window. However after a demanding start, the shingle bank becomes firmer, the result of lorries and trucks flattening it in the course of providing materials for coastal defence work hereabouts. When I walked this section, a small area of the bank had been closed and an impressive mass of boulders was being accumulated for this purpose. While East Head and a goodly section of the coast path between there and East Wittering is popular with walkers, you may not meet any other walkers along this section at all. The shingle bank remains surprisingly good to walk on, the views to the hills above Chichester, including the Trundle and Goodwood, as well as to the Isle of Wight, are excellent, and you can also train your binoculars on passing shipping and back to the distant buildings of Portsmouth. At length you come to the end of the shingle bank, your way ahead blocked by a large brick house, Romona. It's not possible, even at low tide, to keep to the beach here, so veer left along a metalled road which services the West Sands Caravan Park, and continue along it in the same south-easterly direction, keeping Romona and then chalets to the right. The metalled road bends sharp left and as it does so, carry straight on to regain the shingle bank. Now, continue along the resumed shingle bank, passing Medmerry Mill which is to your left.

The early 19th century Medmerry Mill on the approach to Selsey

Medmerry Mill

This simple brick tower mill, described by Arthur Mee as "stately," has been known both as Selsey Mill and Medmerry Mill. Mills have existed on or near this site for well over 300 years, and the present one dates back to 1820. Its fan and sails were removed in 1936 but, having fallen into a dilapidated state thereafter, it was restored, with restoration being completed in 1961 and a new set of sails being fitted in 1977. Flour was milled here until 1910, and the old machinery was then replaced and for a while was available for cracking beans and rolling oats. It ended its working life somewhat ingloriously in the 1920's, no longer milling flour but grinding pepper!

At length the going eases as you join a good path that takes you round the edge of low cliffs. At the end of this very short cliff walk, you turn right on to a gravel drive which goes forward to West Street, where you must briefly forsake the sea. Turn left and follow West Street away from the sea, then turn first right into Clayton Road, an unremarkable residential road. Look out for Warner Road, the second turning on the right off Clayton Road. Turn right down Warner Road and you will find yourself by the shore once again. On reaching the shore, turn left to follow a good path, taking you to the end of Hillfield Road. This is the closest you get to the centre of Selsey. By detouring left up Hillfield Road you will reach the High Street and its shops in ten minutes.

Selsey

Selsey once stood on an island, known as Seal Island, and for centuries it was only accessible by ferry. Even today only one road properly links it with the outside world. It was in AD 681 that St Wilfrid arrived at Selsey, and he subsequently built both a cathedral and a monastery here. Although the bishopric was moved to Chichester in 1070 in order to comply with the requirement to relocate episcopal sees to urban centres, it saw 23 bishops in its

Shingle dominates throughout the walk between East Wittering and Selsey

lifespan of roughly 350 years. Neither the monastery nor the cathedral building were to survive; the cathedral, sadly, was to be but one casualty of the constantly rising waters. The fact of Selsey being the most southerly spot on the Sussex coast has made it especially vulnerable to potential invaders; gun batteries were erected here during the Napoleonic Wars, and in the Second World War Selsey became a minor naval base with many sections of Mulberry Harbour, which played a key role in the D-day landings, kept here.

The sea has not been all bad news for Selsey; among many trades and industries that have flourished here, the town has had and still enjoys a prosperous fishing industry, with the surrounding waters providing a prodigious variety of fish including most famously the Selsey cockle. However, Selsey has never enjoyed the garishness and bright lights of other South Coast resorts. There are many buildings of architectural interest, with several made from Mixon limestone quarried from Mixon Reef just off Selsey Bill. The 19th century **St Peter's Church** incorporates much of the old church at Church Norton, about which more below. The old church, save for the chancel, was moved to its present position in the town from Church Norton in 1864, for the convenience of parishioners, and features of the old church which are now in St Peter's include a font that dates back to around 1100, and a section of 15th century nave roofing. The older secular buildings in Selsey include the early 17th century **Sessions Cottage,** the 16th century **Malt House,** and the 16th or 17th century **Homestead,** of red brick and thatch. While some writers have looked with concern on the proliferation of bungalows and holiday homes, it remains a friendly, unassuming place, not certain whether it is in fact a village or a town.

Selsey, however, was put spectacularly on the map by the events of 7th January 1998 when a tornado struck. It lasted just 30 seconds, but left 1000 homes damaged and a repair bill which was estimated to work out at £60,000 per second of its duration.

The coast route continues on a good path, now on the route of the Manhood Way. Look

Selsey's very own pier - the Selsey Lifeboat visitor centre

seawards and enjoy the views back to the Witterings for the last time, for you are now arriving at Selsey Bill, the southernmost point on the whole route. You pass to the seaward side of a large green; if the tide is low, bear right to follow a concrete way which, with the help of some steps and a climb over a low fence, rounds Selsey Bill and scrambles up onto a proper path on its east side. If the tide renders that impossible, veer left at the far corner of the green and follow the signed path which goes away from the sea, passes to the left of Bill Cottage and quickly veers right to the coastal path on what is now the east side of Selsey Bill. Suddenly a brand new vista opens up with extensive views ahead to Pagham Harbour, Aldwick and Bognor Regis. An excellent concrete path means progress north-eastwards away from the Bill, beside the shore, is extremely easy, and only occasionally do small patches of shingle submerge the concrete. There are plenty of seats, many bearing memorial plaques. Soon you pass the boats and noticeboards of Selsey Angling Club and go under a walkway that takes visitors to the Selsey Lifeboat with its all-weather exhibition and gift shop. You continue beyond the lifeboat, still making good fast progress. The views to the left, across a large area of housing known as the East Beach district of Selsey, are uninspiring, but the views forward to Bognor Regis and beyond are splendid. A plaque erected by the council commemorates Eric Coates, who was inspired by this view in 1930 to compose By The Sleepy Lagoon, the theme tune for the ever-popular Desert Island Discs. Beyond the plaque the concrete path finishes and it is now a tough walk across shingle. Progress becomes noticeably slower but the scenery improves, the housing on the left giving way to the pleasant woodland of Park Copse. It is here that you enter Pagham Harbour Nature Reserve, about which more later. Beyond Park Copse, still to your left, is a small lake, and beyond that, look to your left for a green path which provides temporary relief from the shingle. Follow the path in the same direction until you shortly reach a footpath sign, bearing right here up on to the bank again. The going is now somewhat gentler.

Soon you see the waters of Pagham Harbour ahead to your left. There appears to be a clear *way ahead over the shingle between these waters and the sea to your right, but it is deceptive; this is in fact a shingle spit, with no way forward to Bognor Regis. There is a tantalisingly narrow gap between the two shingle embankments which a century ago was one continuous embankment. As it is, you must now head away from the sea to make progress. Just before the incursion of the Pagham Harbour waters to your left, bear left over some wooden sleepers and proceed along a path that goes beside the harbour waters. It is however possible for you to detour along the shingle spit towards the mouth of Pagham Harbour. I really recommend this, if your legs and feet are up to it and time is on your side. There's initially a good firm path through the shingle which brings you to a fence; beyond the fence is a nesting area and you are asked to avoid entering it. Accordingly, if you wish to continue, veer right round the near side of the fence and then at the corner bear left to walk on along the shingle. I suggest you should try and get to the point where you can see the maddeningly narrow harbour mouth, its initial course, and its eventual broadening out. You can enjoy splendid views across to Bognor Regis as well as inland towards the Downs; you also get a bird's eye view of how far you will in fact have to walk to get to Bognor Regis past Pagham and Aldwick, the buildings of which, including the splendid church at Pagham, you can see just over the water. Now simply retrace your steps and proceed to the wooden sleepers. Straight ahead of you is a fine red brick building, Norton Priory; it used to be a rectory, which in turn was supposedly built on the site of Wilfrid's College of Canons. There is Saxon work in the foundations and some medieval work remains in the west portion of the house. The views hereabouts are superb, and Chichester Cathedral, which you last saw just beyond Itchenor, now comes back into view. You pass a slip road leading to Church Norton, and unless you really are pushed for time you should detour up the road to inspect firstly The Mound, an earthwork that is thought to be a Roman coastal defence fort, and then St Wilfrid's Chapel.*

The charming St Wilfrid's Chapel, just a short stroll from the coast path

St Wilfrid's Chapel

Some sources believe the chapel to have been built on the site of St Wilfrid's monastery while others believe that the monastery lay further to the east and that the site has now been submerged by the waters of Pagham Harbour. The present chapel dates from the 13th century and was once much larger than it is today; however in 1864 all but the chancel of the building was removed to St Peter's in Selsey for the convenience of residents. The chancel, which by ecclesiastical law could not be removed, was restored in 1905 and named St Wilfrid's Chapel in 1917. Perhaps the loveliest story associated with the chapel is that of Eddi, St Wilfrid's curate, who according to a poem by Rudyard Kipling rang the bell for midnight mass one very stormy Christmas Eve. No human beings ventured out, and Eddi's congregation consisted of an "old marsh donkey" and a "wet, yoke-weary bullock!"

You continue round the harbour edge; the path remains close to the shore and the going is somewhat slippery in places. However soon you reach a proper embankment path and from now on the walking is very much easier. Apart from one brief interlude when you follow the shore, you remain on an embankment path all the way to the B2145, now heading south-westwards, away from the sea! Just short of the B2145 the path swings right to run parallel with the road and cross the water. Having crossed the water you should NOT go straight ahead through the gate but instead you bear right along a path that stays beside the harbour. Shortly you reach the course of the old Selsey Tram railway, noting the old embankment and bridge abutments to the right. Turn left to follow the course of the railway on a really excellent path.

The Selsey Tram

The Selsey Tram, which opened in 1897, was a remarkable old railway line. It was not actually a tramway at all, but was called a tramway to escape certain legal requirements. The line's engineer was Colonel Stephens, a well-known railway entrepreneur famed for running railways on a shoestring. The Selsey Tram was no exception; there was no signalling, no crossing gates, the most basic system of communication, and very aged rolling stock including one engine which was 58 years old when it came to the Selsey Tram. The line was used by daytrippers and holidaymakers but also conveyed a tremendous amount of freight. Until the First World War the line thrived, with a dozen trains each way per day at its peak round 1913. However its fortunes declined rapidly in the 1920's, chiefly due to the unremitting exodus of traffic, both travellers and freight, to the roads, and it finally closed in January 1935.

The path emerges at Mill Lane, and here your walk along the Selsey Tramway ends. By detouring left and then right on to the B2145 you will reach the straggling village of Sidlesham. There are regular buses to Chichester from the bus stop at the nearby junction of the B2145 with Manhood Lane. However, the coast route turns right on to Mill Lane and follows it beside the water's edge. Your route turns right off Mill Lane just as the lane bends sharp left, the coast path passing immediately to the right of the first buildings beyond the bend. A little further up the lane is the Crab and Lobster pub, which is deservedly very popular with walkers and birdwatchers.

Sidlesham Mill and Pagham Harbour

Despite the name Mill Lane, there is no trace of the mill which once stood here. Built in 1755, it was a tide mill, meaning that its mill wheels were turned by water rushing in on the rising tide; the water was then impounded in the mill pond so it could be released as the tide fell. Sidlesham was once a busy port, shipping out corn from the quay and importing coal and other goods that could not be obtained locally. It came into its own as a port from the 14th century, when severe storms meant that the old port at Pagham effectively ceased to be able to exist, and at one time ships sailed from here to France. Smuggling was rife; one favoured technique of smugglers was to rope together casks of spirits so they floated just below the surface, then allow the tide to bring them to shore. In 1873 the Pagham Harbour Reclamation Act was passed, as a result of which a great barrier across the harbour mouth was built, providing an area of rich alluvial mud which provided excellent farmland. However, the sea was to have the last laugh. In December 1910, a storm caused the new barrier to be breached along a 40-yard stretch, the farmland was flooded and a new Pagham Harbour was created. The newly-formed harbour, with the surrounding shingle, saltmarsh and fields were recognised as being so picturesque and of such value to birdwatchers and nature-lovers that the area was designated as a nature reserve in 1964. It is perhaps most noteworthy for being a visiting place and breeding ground for the little tern, one

Part of the coast path round Pagham Harbour which overlaps with the old
Chichester to Selsey railway, the Selsey Tram.

of Britain's rarest breeding sea birds, but there are many other recorded visitors. There does remain a legacy of stories about the submerged Selsey Tramway while the new embankment across the flooded area was being constructed, passengers having to make do with a substitute "bus" service consisting of a horse-drawn carriage. Some passengers preferred to sit on top of the carriage rather than inside, in order to avoid getting wet when the bus passed through the floods and the floor got drenched; one can only speculate what option was preferred when it was raining!

SECTION 4 - **SIDLESHAM TO LITTLEHAMPTON**

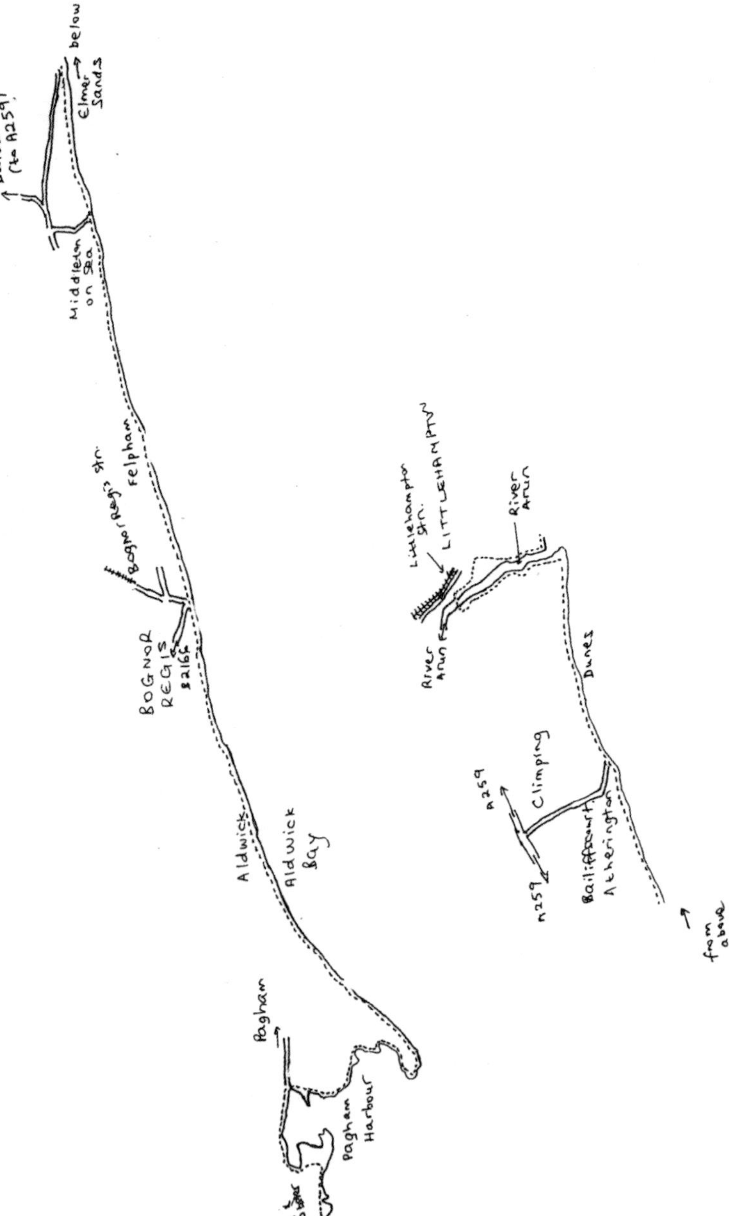

B2132 (to A259)

Elmer below Sands

Middleton on Sea

Felpham

Bognor Regis Stn.

BOGNOR REGIS B2166

Aldwick

Aldwick Bay

Pagham

Pagham Harbour

Littlehampton Stn.

LITTLEHAMPTON

River Arun

River Arun

Dunes

A259

Climping

Bailiffscourt

Atherington

A259

from above

SECTION 4 - SIDLESHAM TO LITTLEHAMPTON

Length:	13 miles (add 2 miles if you have to make all the high tide detours).
Start:	Mill Lane, Sidlesham.
Finish:	Terminus Place, Littlehampton.
Public Transport:	Regular buses serving Bognor Regis on the Brighton-Worthing-Littlehampton-Chichester route (700); regular trains from Bognor Regis to Littlehampton and London via Barnham; regular trains from Littlehampton to Portsmouth, Brighton and London.
Refreshments:	Bognor Regis (P,C,S); Felpham - slightly off route (P,C,S); Climping - off route (P); Littlehampton (P,C,S).
Conditions:	This is a walk of immense contrasts, from gentle harbour-side strolling to shingle tramping, and the reward is a huge variety of landscapes and spectacular views on a clear day. There are a number of sections that are impassable at high tide, and detours will add to your journey time. One high tide obstruction, on the beach on the approach to Bognor, cannot be detoured round, so check tide tables carefully to avoid a lengthy wait.

Having turned right into Mill Lane you follow it briefly, but just before the road bends left, join a signed path leading off to the right, keeping the harbour waters to your right. However, this path floods at high tide in which case you will need to continue along Mill Lane, soon passing and perhaps visiting the hugely popular Crab & Lobster pub (you may of course wish to visit the pub anyway, regardless of the tide!). In a couple of hundred yards, opposite the house Appleporch, bear right onto a signed grassy footpath which soon takes you to the harbourside path. Whichever route you've followed, simply now proceed along the path keeping the harbour waters to your right. This path can be very slippery, muddy and watery in places, and although it's passable here even at high tide, expect to get your boots wet! The going improves a little as the path veers to the left to cut a corner, and you can now clearly see Pagham Wall and Pagham church ahead. However, it's not long before you reach another "high tide" obstacle, a channel which will block your way. If you're blocked, you'll need to retrace your steps to just short of a fence going away from the path to your right as you look back towards Sidlesham. Turn right to walk beside the fence; there's no path as such, but the going through the rough grass is quite safe. Simply walk round until you reach the far side of

The lovely grouping of harbourside houses at Sidlesham includes the popular Crab & Lobster pub

the obstacle then bear left back onto the path. Go forward to reach a junction of paths, turning right and shortly arriving at the embankment and sea defence known as Pagham Wall with an excellent path along the top of the embankment. This is glorious walking and if you have picked a high tide for the journey you can really enjoy it.

The wall ends at the old thatched Salt House (which no longer houses salt) and again the tide will dictate what you do next. Outside high tide, turn right immediately beyond the Salt House down a slipway to proceed beside the shore once more on a signed path past the buildings of Little Welbourne. But at high tide you can't do this: instead, walk straight on up a lane which soon bends sharp left (1) by the vicarage. The lane continues to Pagham Church.

Pagham Church

This has been a holy place for at least 3500 years, and middle Bronze Age burials have been found here. The present church contains a reconstructed Saxon jar in the south aisle, a Norman font, a part-13th century chancel, 13th century nave arcades, and a rose window at the west end which was erected in thanksgiving for the recovery of George V from illness in 1928.

Shortly beyond the left bend referred to at (1) above there's a gap in the hedge to the right; turn right through this gap onto an area of green, and although it's not signed, by following it round to the half right you'll reach a gate beyond which the shoreside path can be accessed. From this point there's a choice of route, either the path along the shore or a parallel green path that's separated from the shore by vegetation and a fence. The former obviously offers the better views but again it gets flooded in places at high tide, so if you've had to follow the diversionary route from the Salt House it's better to stick to the second option to avoid annoying backtracking. In due course the routes unite and whatever the state of the tide it's then a straightforward easy walk which passes just to the harbour side of the caravans of Church Farm Holiday Village and then Pagham Lagoon. Immediately beyond the lagoon bear left onto a shingle track, soon arriving at another track(2) leading to a double gate to the left and a single gate to your right. Now you have a choice. If you're pushed for time, you can cut a large corner, going straight across the shingle along a board walk path to the top of the shingle bank looking down on the open sea, very close to the harbour mouth (3). However, I really recommend that you bear right onto track marked (2) above, continuing beyond the single gate and following it past another lagoon, describing effectively a semi-circle round this second lagoon. When you reach the apex of this semi-circle, stop and enjoy a quite fantastic view back across the harbour including of course St Wilfrid's Chapel, which will seem a very long way back! You can congratulate yourself that this long inland detour has been completed. Complete the semi-circle to arrive at point (3). From here you can clearly see the harbour mouth, invisible all the way up from Selsey by virtue of the shape of the spit. All that detour for little more than 250 yards of water. Now begins a long tramp on the shingle beach beside Aldwick Bay. There is no path or road at the back of the beach; immediately behind the shingle

are the houses and gardens firstly of Pagham and then the Aldwick Bay estate. I suggest you get as far down the beach as the tide will allow you, and, keeping the buildings of Bognor Regis in your sights, march resolutely north-eastwards along the shore. The bay has historically been regarded as strategically important. A gun battery was erected here in 1793 to guard against the threat of French invasion, and sometimes at low tide it is possible to make out a large object straight out to sea; this is a section of Mulberry Harbour which did not

Looking across the waters of Pagham Harbour at high tide. The spire of Pagham Church can just be made out in the distance

make it across to France for the D-day landings. The lower the tide, the greater the chances of your finding firmer patches on which to walk as you do head towards Bognor Regis, and indeed there are small areas of sand among the shingle, but this is certainly tough going. You will have to wait until Park Road (see below) for access into the Aldwick Bay estate or Aldwick itself.

Aldwick

Despite the large Aldwick Bay Estate, built between the two world wars, Aldwick does have some older cottages, a 200-year-old inn called the **Ship** which was said to be connected to the beach by a smugglers' tunnel, and an old tithe barn called **Swingates Barn** which was damaged by fire in 1954. Historically its moment of glory was in 1929 when between 9 February and 15 May George V stayed at the now demolished early 19th century Craigweil House in Aldwick while convalescing from illness. On his deathbed he is reputed to have been offered the chance to revisit the Bognor area, perhaps in the hope that it might revive him, prompting his reputed famous last words, "B***** Bognor!"

You keep on the beach, soon passing a number of lines of rock heading out to sea, but there are no further features to enable you to monitor your progress until you reach a succession of *breakwaters. You negotiate these but, unless the tide is very low, you are then forced to the top of the beach to use steps, then a concrete path, and then more steps to negotiate a huge wall of large rocks. Do not try and climb over the rocks. Note that at very high tide even the steps and concrete path round the rocks may not be usable. Not far beyond the wall of rocks a long line of beach huts becomes visible to the left; when you draw level with the last, climb up through the shingle and you will see a good concrete walkway ahead of you. Follow this promenade beside the sea towards the centre of Bognor Regis. By shortly detouring left into Park Road you will reach Aldwick Road and its shops, offering the first food shopping since Selsey. Staying on the walkway, known as the Esplanade, you soon pass the Bognor Yacht Club, Rock Gardens and the gracious 1830 Royal Norfolk Hotel, all to your left. Moving on, you pass two of the more gracious areas of Bognor on your left hand side, namely the Steyne (its name being derived from "stone" with which the shoreline was once liberally covered) and Waterloo Square, the green in the middle of which was once a patch of grazing land. There is easy access from Waterloo Square into the town centre.*

Bognor Regis

It was a wealthy Southwark hatter, Sir Richard Hotham, who in 1787 made it his mission to convert Bognor into a rival of Bath. Prior to Sir Richard's arrival, Bognor had a reputation as a rather seedy fishing and farming community, but Sir Richard began to transform the place, investing £100,000 to provide 40 new buildings, and

The tantalisingly narrow mouth of Pagham Harbour

encouraging Royalty to visit. Although the reigning King George III was never seduced by its new-found charms, the only child of the future King George IV, Charlotte, spent some summers here. It is possible still to admire Sir Richard's buildings, including the Dome (part of Bognor's higher education institute) and **Hotham House,** set in lovely gardens and built by Sir Richard for his own occupancy; both date back to around 1790. After Sir

Richard's death in 1799, it became difficult to convince folk to invest in Bognor, but an "improvement company" did persuade some speculators to do so, and the Steyne and **Waterloo Square** were the result. Following the departure of George V and Queen Mary after their stay in the vicinity, the town's authorities were informed that they had Royal permission to add "Regis" to the town's name.

By 1850, Bognor's population was still only 2000, but in 1864 the railway arrived in the town and it quickly became a much more popular holiday destination. A pier was completed the very next year, boasting a 1000ft jetty; the toll was 1d with 4d for bathchairs! Early in the 20th century, two huge entertainment centres were built: the Kursaal, which opened in 1910 and included shops, a theatre, skating rink and tea-room, and also the Pavilion. Opened in the summer of 1922, it was used for dances, plays and exhibitions, but was demolished in 1949. The Kursaal was renamed the Rex Entertainment Centre and was demolished in 1975, to be succeeded by the Regis Centre. Despite its excellent sunshine records, the town has had its share of dreadful weather, with many storms which have caused much damage and flooding. As recently as 28 October 2000 a tornado with speeds of 120mph struck the town, causing damage to more than 100 homes and leaving five people injured. During a storm in 1820, the sea broke into a seafront theatre during a performance, and it is said that the actors and the audience had to be taken out in boats!

Although the shopping centre is soulless and dull, many visitor attractions remain today, including the Alexandra Theatre, contained within the Regis Centre, and also the verdant Hotham Park which draws lots of visitors and residents in summer. Two annual events continue to form an important part of Bognor Regis' menu of entertainment, namely the Clowns' Convention and the Birdman Rally, where numerous competitors test out all kinds of ingenious devices to fly gracefully off the pier. Finally there is of course Butlins, which arrived in 1960 and remains an immensely popular family attraction.

Continuing along the Esplanade, you will soon reach the pier to your right, with its amusement arcade, souvenir shops and nightclub, then beyond the pier you continue along the front, passing a number of kiosks. You carry on along the Esplanade east of the pier; on your left, across the road, is the modern Alexandra Theatre and the 1929 Town Hall, a sturdy red-brick Georgian-style building. And with that, you start to pull away from Bognor

Looking across the shingle to Bognor pier

Regis and head towards Felpham, passing Butlins with its unmistakable frothy white roof.

Felpham

Felpham's most notable building is the **Church of St Mary,** with a 15th century church tower and other features that date back to the 12th and 13th centuries. Felpham, which should properly be pronounced Fel-fam, has many attractive old cottages including the red brick **Manor House** on Limmer Lane which dates back to the 17th century. In that century the village could boast ten different trades and 42 tradesmen. The village's most famous resident was the poet William Blake, who came here in September 1800 and stayed for exactly three years. His cottage, once known as Rose Cottage, is situated, quite appropriately, in Blake's Lane, and is an attractive building of thatch and flint.

Continuing along the front beyond Sea Road, you pass the sturdy flint-built Beachcroft Hotel and continue past the Felpham Sailing Club (attached to a somewhat unsightly cafe) and a rather ugly proliferation of beach huts nearby. The surroundings now become more genteel as trim suburban houses and gardens line the left-hand side of your route. At length the concrete promenade ends, being replaced firstly by a dirt-track and then a more stony, shingly path, but another twist to the left brings you to a pleasant area of green which you walk across.
The public right of way which has continued along the coast since you reached Bognor Regis ends here, and progress onwards does depend on the state of the tide. For the next couple of hundred yards, there is no shingle bank, and nothing between the sands and high stone walls protecting the adjacent houses from the wrath of the sea. At high tide, there may be no way forward and it will be necessary either to wait for the sea to retreat, or make a road detour. This is described below. DO NOT ATTEMPT TO CLIMB ALONG OR OVER THE WALLS. Outside high tide, you will have no problem, passing to the seaward end of the walls and proceeding along the sands. Shortly you find yourself walking parallel with a shingle bank to your left, and if the tide is rising you can retreat to the bank and proceed reasonably easily along that. Soon you pass to the right of an imposing block of modern flats, necessarily sturdy looking and not unpleasing to the eye, and from then on there is a firmer path along the back of the bank. If you choose to remain on the sands, the walking - after negotiation of a few breakwaters - is excellent. You are now on what is known as Elmer Sands, with a succession of rock-built groynes separating you from the sea. A plaque on the shingle bank advises that this forms part of a coastal defence scheme opened in September 1993. Just beyond the fifth groyne watch for a flight of wooden steps to your left, and use these to climb on to the bank to join an excellent path heading on eastwards. Look backwards to enjoy what, on a clear day, is a superb view that extends to Selsey Bill and the Isle of Wight. To your left, and below you, is a little green, with the houses of Elmer beyond it.
If high tide has forced you away from the sea at Sea Lane, turn left up this lane, a pleasant street of flint-built and thatched houses, turning right at the T-junction at the end on to Middleton Road with its shops. You follow Middleton Road as far as the mini-roundabout. Go straight across the mini-roundabout into Elmer Road and follow it past the 19th century **St Nicholas Church.** *At length you reach a gate which separates Elmer Road from Manor Road. Turn right immediately before the gate along a little road which brings you back to the shore. Turn left and you will shortly reach the flight of wooden steps with the green on the left. The road detour adds a good extra mile to the journey.*
There now follows a delightful stretch along an excellent path. At last the houses relent on the left, and the walk becomes truly rural in every sense, with the sea to your right and fields and woodlands to the left. The track drops slightly and bends a little to the left, passing a small area of woodland and a house called Poole Place. The going is straightforward, and reasonably

kind to the feet, as you proceed along the top of the shingle bank, keeping a small pond and fields to your left. Ahead of you there is one particularly conspicuous tower block which signifies the proximity of your next big resort, Littlehampton, but nearer to hand, and rather more attractive, is the sight of a line of sand dunes just to the west of this town. Soon the buildings of Bailiffscourt, a mock-medieval house of warm limestone built in 1935, become visible on the left, and you arrive at Atherington, passing the huge car park at the end of the road coming down from the A259 through Climping. This road contains several good barns and flint cottages including Brookpits, a good example of a 17th century yeoman's house. Bailiffscourt, now an hotel, is certainly the grandest building along the road.

Beyond the end of the Climping road you continue along the back of the beach, having to veer slightly left and scramble a little higher up the shingle to make progress. Having paused to enjoy the wonderful view towards the Downs, and in particular Arundel Castle and Cathedral, you have to endure some tough going initially along the shingle, but after a few hundred yards the

surface becomes firmer. It is then an easy walk all the way to West Beach at the mouth of the Arun, along a good path that hugs the dunes; you have the shingle bank to your right, and the dunes to your left. Alternatively, at low tide, you can walk along the sands. In prehistoric times, the sea was a mile further out, and settlers came here to hunt and fish, digging rifes to drain the marshes. Birds to be seen hereabouts include the kestrel, sanderling, finch, tit, thrush, turnstone, ringed plover and

Sodden sands following high tide at Middleton-on-Sea

oystercatcher, the sea yields crabs, cockles, whelks, shrimps and cuttlefish, stones on the shore may include rough periwinkle, and plant life includes sea kale and birds' foot trefoil. It is quite a surprise, after walking along what seems a fairly isolated stretch of coastline, to arrive at an area of metal fencing with the urban sprawl of Littlehampton immediately ahead of you. Separating you from it is the River Arun, which here flows into the sea after meandering through miles of glorious Sussex countryside. At the fencing you turn left and begin walking up the west bank of the Arun, almost at once passing a car park and a useful refreshment hut. Having exited from the car park, you can fork right on to a little beach right by the river bank, but once you have passed the boat house you are forced back on to the road; it may be just as easy to follow the road from the car park. A parallel path is available, as you pass a large assembly of boats separating you from the river. Soon you pass the golf clubhouse which is to your left, and here a concrete path forks right off the road. Take this path, which provides a pleasant walk reasonably close to the riverbank, with views across to Littlehampton. In due course the path is reunited with the road, called Rope Walk, and you follow the road in the same direction, going forward to a T-junction. Turn right here and cross the footbridge over the river. Formerly there was a swing bridge here; constructed at a cost of £13,000, it was opened by the Duke of Norfolk in 1908 and was floodlit by 1200 candle-power lamps. It was demolished in 1980 and replaced in 1981 by the present construction which cost half a million pounds to build.

Once over the bridge you turn immediately right into River Road. Follow this for a couple of hundred yards, ignoring a left turn into Purbeck Place and reaching a crossroads junction with Mariners Quay going off to the right and Terminus Place to the left. This section ends here. The coastal route turns right into Mariners Quay, while to access the centre of Littlehampton, turn left and follow Terminus Place. This almost immediately reaches the railway station; to reach the town centre, turn right at the T-junction by the station and follow the road to arrive at the main precinct.

Littlehampton

Littlehampton is one of those settlements on the Sussex coast that has enjoyed prosperity as a port, as a workaday place and as a holiday resort. It was an important port in Saxon times, and in the Middle Ages was a landing place for Caen stone from Normandy which was used in churches and secular buildings throughout Sussex. The harbour was regularly visited by ships carrying coal from northern England and by vessels with cargoes of timber from the Baltic. During the 19 years that followed the arrival of the railway in 1863, there was a cross-Channel ferry link between Littlehampton and Honfleur in France. The principal traffic of these steamers was not passengers but freight. Huge quantities of both perishable and durable goods passed through the port, and the discovery of oyster beds off the shore of Littlehampton led to huge numbers of fishing boats congregating in the harbour. Gradually the importance of Littlehampton as a port declined, but it remains a base for pleasure cruises up the Arun, fishing and the dredging of marine aggregates.

Littlehampton has also been an important base for shipbuilding, with Littlehampton ships - and seafarers - sailing all over the world. Over time the demand for wooden sailing vessels declined, but in the 20th century the shipyards flourished in the production of other craft, including fast gunboats that were manufactured during the 1939-45 war, motor yachts and lifeboats; Osborne's, opened in 1919, is one of the country's major lifeboat builders. One particular milestone in the history of shipbuilding in Littlehampton came with the construction by Harvey's in the 1870's of the 532-ton Trossachs, which took sheep and shepherds to the Falklands, helping to create what became the staple industry of these islands. During both world wars, Littlehampton turned from a seaside resort into an important military base, and the town itself has expanded radically since, with considerable residential and industrial development.

Sea bathing began at Littlehampton in the 1750's, and over the next eighty years or so it began to be seen by writers, artists and others as a secluded, unspoilt place to enjoy the sea. The town's first real entrepreneur was Peter le Cocq, but his influence, unlike that of Sir Richard Hotham in Bognor, did not extend to the establishment of an elegant coastal watering place, and certainly the town never became a centre of architectural excellence. However, the end of the 18th and beginning of the 19th century saw considerable building here; in 1790 the fifth earl of Berkeley decided to build a seaside residence at the east end of the **Green,** while le Cocq himself built a coffee house which was to become the Beach Hotel. **Norfolk Place** and **South Terrace** soon followed, and from a cluster of flint and brick houses in the 18th century Littlehampton was to become very much bigger as the 19th century progressed. The railway's arrival helped to turn the town into an exceedingly popular resort; its population, just 584 in 1801, had risen to 5954 in 1901. Amongst those who came to Littlehampton in the 19th century were Lord Byron, John Constable and Samuel Taylor Coleridge. Littlehampton has continued to prosper as a pleasant, if unsophisticated, resort ever since. The development of the town as a resort did not please everybody. The town mill was demolished in 1932 to make way for Butlins amusement park which opened in the following year, and townsfolk dismissed the new complex as "Whoopee City!"

Part of the precious countryside gap between Middleton-on-Sea and Littlehampton

SECTION 5 - **LITTLEHAMPTON TO LANCING**

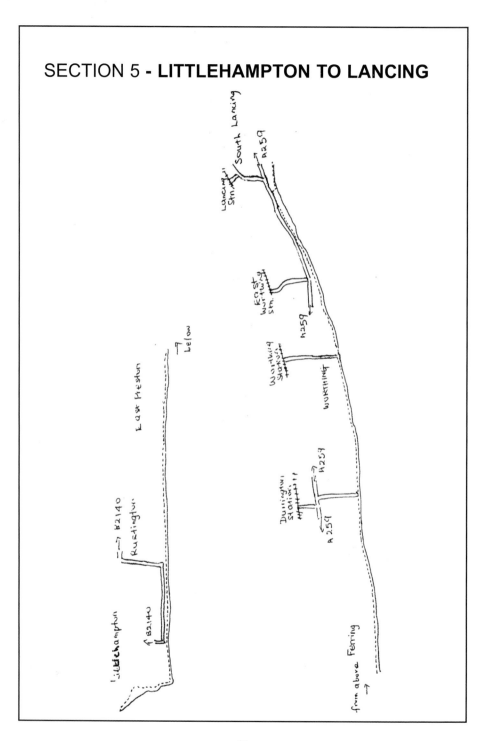

SECTION 5 - LITTLEHAMPTON TO LANCING

Length:	10.5 miles.
Start:	Junction of River Road with Terminus Place and Mariners Quay, Littlehampton.
Finish:	Junction of A259 with Bessborough Terrace, Lancing.
Public Transport:	Regular trains serving Goring-by-Sea, Durrington-on-Sea, Worthing and Lancing on the Portsmouth-Brighton line.
Refreshments:	East Preston (P,C,S); Ferring (P,C,S); Goring (P,C,S); Worthing (P,C,S); Lancing (P,C,S).
Conditions:	This is a really easy straightforward walk with only two comparatively short sections of shingle and no high tide diversions. A fit walker will complete it in three hours or less. It is however much more urban in character than any section so far, and although the open sea is your constant companion to your right, most of the time you will have houses or flats to your left.

From the crossroads junction of River Road with Terminus Place and Mariners Quay, follow Mariners Quay and go forward along an alleyway to reach a waterfront walk. Turn left to follow it past impressive new housing developments along the east bank of the Arun, and keeping the river to your right, continue past a café and onto a pavement beside Pier Road. Continue along the promenade between Pier Road and the river to reach the river mouth, passing a huge fun park and the Windmill Entertainment Centre before turning sharp left to join the seafront promenade.

Before striding out eastwards, take one last look out at Littlehampton's pier and also the lighthouse, built in 1948 to replace a mid-19th century "pepper-pot" lighthouse. Having done so, you head resolutely along the promenade with the open sea once again to your right and a broad expanse of green to your left, separating you from the centre of the town. At the Norfolk Gardens Pleasure Park you are joined by a road which runs parallel with you to your left, and for a while beachhuts separate the promenade from the sea. You may wish to traipse along the shingle instead, or the sand at low tide. The beach huts relent and the sea views are again uninterrupted from the promenade; across the road to the left is firstly a big sports complex, and then the Rustington Convalescent Home, a fine Wren-style redbrick house dating back to 1897 and set in attractive grounds. Around here the promenade effectively ends, and you find yourself walking along what is simply a pavement beside Sea Road, with large areas of modern housing now immediately opposite without any intervening stretches of green. Looking back you can enjoy lovely views to the dunes, and you may also see the dome of Butlins poking out on the horizon. Shortly after the promenade becomes a mere pavement, Sea Road swings sharply to the left. Your way is straight ahead, along a paved path across an area of green, but by detouring along Sea Road you will reach the centre of Rustington. It's quite a long walk, but it is worth the detour.

Rustington

Although Rustington is one of a number of settlements along the Sussex coast that have been overrun with 20th century development, there is evidence of life here in prehistoric times, and finds here include flint tools, implements and ancient pots, cooking vessels, glass and coins, and traces of a Roman tide mill. The name Rustington is of Saxon origin; the Saxon who built his farmstead ("tun") here is believed to be nicknamed Rusta, perhaps because he had red hair! As you proceed up the road (Sea Road turning into Sea Lane) you will arrive at a junction with The Street, and on the corner there is a fine **parish church.** Its west tower dates back to the late 12th century, and there is also a 13th century chancel and north transept. On the north face of the tower is an ancient clock, previously at Great Bedwyn in Wiltshire but rescued from a cottage garden scrapheap, bought for £2 and repositioned at its present site. Beyond the church is Rustington's excellent shopping centre, which has a pleasantly villagey

feel about it, and there are some good cottages of flint and thatch to be found amongst the proliferation of new housing.

For centuries the village was essentially a farming community and it was the advent of the railway in 1846 and consequently quick journey times from London that led to more residents and visitors descending on this hitherto quiet spot. The population of the village was still only 616 in 1901, but during the 20th century there was something of an explosion in development, and over the century it rose to 12,500. The village was catering not only for residents but for the holiday trade, and in 1936 the Lido, a first class holiday complex, was established in the village, including a ballroom, lecture hall, floodlit swimming

The Dome Cinema, Worthing's most distinctive seafront attraction, built in 1910

pool, roller skating rink, bowling green and tennis courts. It was demolished in 1968. Today, Rustington has become effectively a suburb of Littlehampton, striving to keep an identity of its own despite its endless trim streets of modern housing. Finally, it should be worth noting Sir Hubert Parry lived in Knightscroft House, a large red tiled Victorian building in Sea Lane, from 1879 until his death in 1918.

You follow the paved path which proceeds pleasantly across a green. The green ends and you then need to cross an area of shingle before picking up a further paved path which heads eastwards towards some beach huts. You are now embarking on a succession of greenswards - areas of immaculate green for public and recreational use, which run between the very private and very exclusive housing to your left, and the sea to your right. To begin with, you are separated from the sea by beach huts, but they soon relent and the walking becomes quite delightful. You then have a choice. The greensward leading to Sea Lane at the south-western end of East Preston is separated from the sea by a tall strip of vegetation, and in order to stay by the sea you will need to forsake soft green for tough shingle. You may prefer the comfort of the green, from which in any case there are many glimpses of the sea through the bushes, and also glimpses to some extremely fine houses to the left. In due course you reach Sea Lane, from which there is convenient access to Angmering station via Sea Lane, Vicarage Lane and Station Road. You bear slightly right on to Sea Lane, then immediately left on to the shingle. You follow the shingle, passing a small boatyard; by detouring left off the shingle into Sea Road you will gain access to East Preston.

East Preston

East Preston is similar to Rustington in many ways; it is a large sprawling community of mostly 20th century housing, with just occasional pockets of older building among the new. The village does boast the fine **Church of St Mary the Virgin,** an early English building with its remarkably thin tower, added around 1500, with an internal width of no more than 6 feet. The stone spire is one of only very few in the county. The north doorway of the church, of Caen stone and oak, dates back to 1130, the nave of the church dates back to the 12th century and there is a 13th century chancel.

The shingle bank broadens out and as it does so you will be able to bear left to join another greensward, with firstly the houses of West Kingston and then Kingston Gorse to your left. When the tide is out, there is a magnificent expanse of sand which you can walk along instead. The sands are fascinating with their many rocks, pools and channels, and you will also be able to see a small collection of black rocks which are visible half a mile offshore at low tide. These are believed to contain the remains of Kingston Chapel which were submerged by the sea in the 17th century; the chapel is thought to have stood on land called Ruston Park where elm trees flourished You pass through two gates in close succession then immediately join another greensward. This ends and you are then faced with another shingle walk past a cafe and some beach huts. Beyond the beach huts look out for a nice paved path, Pattersons Walk, at the back of the beach. This takes you past the village of Ferring. You continue along Pattersons Walk - a mini-promenade is available for a short stretch of it - and arrive at a car park at the south-east end of Ferring, and the western end of the Marine Drive Open Space. The pier and buildings of Worthing are now clearly visible ahead. There is access to the centre of Ferring both via West Drive at the village's west end, and Sea Lane at its east end.

Ferring

Ferring is, like Rustington, a flint village swallowed up in seaside housing. It is, however, an immaculately kept village, boasting a genteel air of peace and tranquillity; there are many attractive gardens fronting the modern houses, there is a nice little shopping centre which at the time of writing included a tiny coffee shop, and a few hundred yards north of the shops is **St Andrew's Church.** This is a neat early English building which dates back to 1250, with an interior full of tablets to the Henty and Olliver families.

The Steyne Gardens, arguably the most gracious part of Worthing

If the tide is out, it is perfectly possible to follow the sands all the way from Ferring to Worthing; this is an easy walk on firm sand. If the tide is in, or you prefer to be further inland, you may continue eastwards from Ferring across a green with Marine Drive to your left. Look northwards and enjoy the excellent view to Highdown Hill with its Iron Age hillfort. It is nice to have a view northwards which is uncluttered by building, but make the most of it; it won't happen again until well beyond Brighton. Continuing east, you soon pick up a good path along the right hand edge of the green, and this continues past a shelter. Beyond the shelter you keep an area of green to your left but the houses begin again across the green. Some bushes occasionally obscure your view of the sea, and for a little while the path weaves its way through these bushes. Beyond the bushes - note also the odd boat "parked" on the shingle to your right - the path swings to the left, and allows you a good view up Sea Lane to the spire of Goring Church. This is as near as you get to Goring-by-Sea, which is something of a misnomer as the village centre is some way back from the sea. The beach here was however mentioned as a smugglers' beach in 1394; the shallow sloping beach and - in those days - only a few scattered houses made Goring *the perfect site for smuggling. The naturalist Richard Jefferies lived out his last few months in Goring in a house called Sea View, which has been re-named Jefferies House in his honour. As you move east of Sea Lane, your path becomes a proper concrete way. You pass an impressively sturdy cafe - a wooden structure on a brick base - then head resolutely towards Worthing. Do look left to Banstead Close, shortly beyond Sea Lane, where there is a fine assembly of palm trees, and on a clear day you can enjoy good northward views to the South Downs beyond Worthing. The metalled path is for a while separated from the sea by beach huts - you may prefer to follow the shingle to the seaward side of the huts - but the huts relent soon after the path passes to the right of a large boatyard. Just at this point there is a small car park and public toilet block which is situated at the bottom of Sea Place, a road which provides easy access to Durrington-on-Sea and its railway station. Like Goring, the centre of Durrington is nowhere near the sea! The walkway widens to become a proper seafront promenade, with a road running parallel with it to your left. At length you reach the pier, and by detouring left on to South Street, directly across the road from the pier, you will get to the busy shopping centre of Worthing, the largest town on the West Sussex coast.*

Worthing

Just like Bognor and Littlehampton, Worthing was a fishing village until the latter part of the 18th century, and in fact had obtained a charter during the reign of Edward III for a market in the 14th century. During the 18th century, however, the increasing patronage of Brighton by Royalty began to influence adjacent areas. In 1798 Princess Amelia, the 15th and last child of George III, visited Worthing and gave it her Royal seal of approval, and also at around this time there were visits from Princess Charlotte, daughter of the Prince Regent, as well as noblemen that included the Duke of Bedford, and the Earls of Warwick, Egremont and Montague. In 1803 Worthing was granted town status; at that time its population was just 2500 but was to rise to 14,500 by 1890. During the early 19th century, just as at Bognor and Littlehampton, some fine building took place as the popularity of Worthing for both residents and visitors increased. Public buildings of importance included the 1812 **St Paul's Church,** with its four column Greek Doric portico, the 1834 Grecian-style old Town Hall, and arguably Worthing's finest building, the theatre in Ann Street, dating back to 1807. Sadly it closed as a theatre in 1855 and towards the end of the 20th century it had become a warehouse! Many splendid houses were however built in the early 19th century which still survive as residences or offices today, with examples of architecture of that period in **Liverpool Terrace, Park Crescent, Montague Place, Bedford Row, Montague Street** and **the Steyne.** Around this time the zest for new building faltered, but the arrival of the railway in 1845 brought many more people to the town and there emerged a different kind of resort from Brighton, offering what has been quaintly described as "quiet domestic joys!"

The late 19th and early 20th centuries saw the town's development as a traditional seaside resort. It was advertised, and has continued to be advertised ever since, as being

Worthing's museum and art gallery in Chapel Road; to visit it requires a brisk walk from the seafront!

especially safe for sea bathing, with a very sunny fog-free climate, but without the garishness or rowdiness of Brighton. It attracted a wide spectrum of visitors, including Oscar Wilde who wrote *The Importance of Being Earnest* here in the 1890's whilst on holiday, and named the hero of the play, John Worthing, after the town. A pier was opened in the 1860's, with a jetty that was restricted to "promenaders only," but the structure was replaced by a much grander one in July 1889. A fine cast iron **band stand** was erected eight years later, and in 1909 mixed bathing was introduced. This had been frowned upon in the Victorian era, although in the late 18th and early 19th century, bathers had often gone into the water stark naked. 1892 saw more than 3000 people attending the town's regatta, with attractions on the beach including conjurers, jugglers and fortune-tellers, while beach lovers in the early years of the 20th century might enjoy sailing, rowing, steamers, donkey rides, ponies and even goat carts which remained a common feature on the shore until 1920. Worthing's long fishing traditions were maintained by the existence of a fish market on the beach, and even today you may find fish being sold from a kiosk on the front. At Easter 1910 the **Dome Cinema** was opened, and it remains a distinctive feature on the sea front to this day. The neo-Georgian **Town Hall,** built to replace the old Grecian-style hall, was opened in 1933 by Prince George, later the Duke of Kent, and contains beautiful pastel coloured mosaics with maritime themes, while the museum is particularly noteworthy for its early nineteenth century paintings, with especially fine Victorian watercolours.

Despite the prosperity which came to Worthing during the 19th and early 20th centuries, the town had its share of troubles during that time. The town's first lifeboat was launched in 1853, but that did not stop the dreadful tragedy of August 1858 when thirteen people, some children, drowned as a result of the fishing boat Mary Eliza capsizing off the coast hereabouts. In March 1913 the promenade part of the pier, reconstructed just 24 years previously, was destroyed by a storm, leaving the pavilion at the sea end completely cut off. The promenade was reconstructed and re-opened in May 1914, but in September 1933 a fire broke out in the pavilion and destroyed that.

The splendid St Paul's Church in Worthing, dating back over two hundred years

The 1880's saw the infamous Worthing riots, arising from the advent of the Salvation Army in the town. A group called the Skeleton Army was formed to oppose them, and considerable unrest resulted. The riots attracted nationwide media coverage, and prompted a cartoon in the satirical journal *Punch*.
Worthing has continued to expand during the 20th century. The town suffered very badly during the Second World War, and during the post war period there was a substantial amount of demolition of both old and even listed buildings. Today the town has many flourishing societies and organisations for all ages, but has become particularly popular with older folk, and perhaps it is small wonder that the town has been nicknamed "God's waiting room!"

Assuming you keep to the promenade, you pass the Dome and the Steyne Gardens, overlooked by the Chatsworth and Ardington Hotels. Look out also for the Boer War memorial. The promenade swings a little to the left; a sign indicates that a small area of the seafront has been reserved "for the delivery of sermons and public speeches! " The promenade continues away from the centre of Worthing - then having twisted slightly left once more passes an assembly of boats and near the Windsor Lodge turns into a pavement beside the horrendously busy A259. You can avoid the road noise by sticking to the beach or indeed the shingle as far as Western Road. Unfortunately even this option becomes unavailable beyond Western Road, because there is an area of private beach which extends right down to the mean low water mark, and you are forced back to the road, passing to the landward side of a row of houses that includes a pink mock-Tudor house named Boleyn. You are now arriving in Lancing. You pass a prominent row of red brick cottages across the road to your left - note the nice old-fashioned sign bearing the words BESSBOROUGH TERRACE! - and shortly beyond Beach Lodge you turn right by a telephone box on to a concrete footpath which heads beachwards again. You can detour to the modern centre of Lancing by continuing briefly along the road and then turning left on to South Street. Lancing's railway station is situated just off South Street.

Lancing

Lancing has been labelled the largest village in Sussex, although with its population of 17,000 many regard it as a town. It is thought to have got its name from Wlencing, one of the sons of Ella, founder of the South Saxon Kingdom. Lancing was historically regarded as a horticultural community, the produce from its market gardens being grapes, peaches, tomatoes, cucumbers, figs and melons, although it supported a brickmaking industry from 1888 until 1913 when the claypits became exhausted. The original centre of Lancing was at what is now known as North Lancing, over a mile from the coast and today accessible only by crossing the busy A27. It boasts a church, parts of which date back to the 12th century, and a cluster of old houses including one, known as Old Cottage, where Charles II is once said to have stayed. The most impressive building in Lancing, again across the A27, is its **College Chapel,** founded in 1848 by Nathaniel Woodard. Those anxious to make progress along the coast, however, will probably only have time to see South Lancing, which is almost entirely modern. As at so many other places along the Sussex coast, smuggling posed a real problem for the authorities here, with tea and brandy being especially popular cargoes. In the first quarter of the 19th century, Coastguard Cottages were built along what is now Lower Brighton Road to combat the menace of smuggling. The coastguards were on duty continuously here; of the two rows of cottages (since demolished), the ones at the back were known as Dreadnought Cottages, for bachelors, while the ones at the front were occupied by married men.

The 19th century saw the menace of smuggling diminish, while the coming of the railway in 1845 helped enhance the popularity of the area as a seaside resort, albeit on a much smaller scale than at Worthing. Visitors to Lancing included the author Evelyn Waugh, who rented a property called the Cliff. People still enjoy its fine sands today, and may be fortunate enough to purchase fresh fish on the seafront. Cooke writes that South Lancing is a "quiet little seaside resort beloved of invalids and avoided by the tripper," referring presumably to the establishment of convalescent homes here in June 1890. They were started by a William Chorley as an auxiliary to a gospel mission, in the hope that the change of scene and fresh sea air would improve the well-being of people from depressed inner-city areas. The inmates of one of the homes wore a uniform of rough navy-blue serge, and were known locally as Chorley's Blue Birds!

The stark coastal scene between Worthing and Lancing

SECTION 6 - **LANCING TO BRIGHTON**

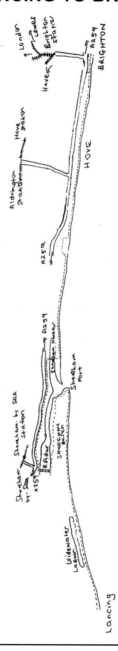

SECTION 6 - LANCING TO BRIGHTON

Length:	11 miles (including Shoreham Harbour detour).
Start:	Junction of A259 with Bessborough Terrace, Lancing.
Finish:	Brighton Pier.
Public Transport:	Regular trains serving Shoreham-by-Sea, Southwick, Hove and Brighton on the Portsmouth-Brighton line; numerous buses serving the 700 route between Worthing and Brighton via Shoreham-by-Sea.
Refreshments:	Shoreham-by-Sea (P,C,S); Hove (P,C,S); Brighton (P,C,S).
Conditions:	This walk could hardly be described as pretty, passing several densely populated areas and industrial workings. There is one particularly tough piece of shingle walking, and there is another messy section between Shoreham Harbour and Hove. However there are numerous features of interest and your journey culminates in arrival in Brighton, the most vibrant and exciting location on the Sussex coast. Make sure you allow plenty of time to enjoy all the city has to offer.

Continue along the concrete path away from South Lancing, which passes the Mermaid cafeteria and then a line of beach huts. Few things are more depressing than gazing along the back end of a line of beach huts, so you may wish to stick to the shingle along here! In due course you resume an uninterrupted view towards the sea, and there are good views to the Downs and Lancing College Chapel to your left. You pass Lancing Sailing Club and a big caravan park, but soon afterwards there is the much more pleasing prospect of the Widewater Lagoon to your left.

Widewater Lagoon
This shallow saline lagoon is situated on marshland formed by sediments that were deposited by the River Adur. The water became isolated when a southern shingle bank developed through a combination of storms and longshore drift. Later it was reinforced artificially, with a second bank being constructed to the north; it is principally fed by sea water permeating through the cracks in the thin clay bed. It is now a fine nature reserve, with plants which include sea anemone, sea campion, sea kale, sea thrift and vipers bugloss, and birds which include redshank, pied wagtail, black-headed gull,

The 12th century St Mary de Haura in Shoreham, one of the finest religious buildings on the Sussex coast

swan, mallard, ringed plover, grey heron and kestrel.

Having passed the lagoon, you continue along the concrete as it veers to the left, becoming West Beach Road. From here the best option is not to remain on the concrete but to climb on to the shingle bank and follow the shingle beach. This stays parallel with West Beach Road, which turns into Kings Walk and then Beach Road; you may of course prefer to stick to the concrete, but it makes for uninspiring walking, particularly as Beach Road becomes separated from the shore by a line of houses that form part of the large Shoreham Beach estate. The walk along the beach is tough going, reminiscent of the long haul from Pagham Lagoon to Bognor Regis, but the reward is arriving at the far end of Shoreham Beach and getting a grandstand view of the mouth both of Shoreham Harbour and the river Adur - so named in the 16th century to support the supposed identification of the Roman town Portus Adurni with Shoreham. Here you will see the rather sad-looking ruins of Shoreham Fort.

Shoreham Beach, Bungalow Town and Shoreham Fort

The Shoreham Beach estate developed from an unplanned collection of bungalows, railway carriages and shacks used originally as holiday dwellings and known as Bungalow Town. Between 1914 and the mid-1920's, it became a favoured venue for early film-makers who set up studios here, attracted by the pure south coast air and the quality of the light. About 20 films were made on Shoreham Beach. Not only filmmakers but a number of actors and music hall performers were based in Bungalow Town, undeterred by the fact that access by road was difficult and amenities were limited; until the Church of the Good Shepherd opened in July 1913, services would be held on the beach, with one service taken by the Bishop of Chichester drawing a congregation of about 200. Celebrities who spent time here included Hetty King, the famous male impersonator of *All The Nice Girls Love A Sailor* fame, and Marie Loftus, known as the Sarah Bernhardt of music halls. Their accommodation was surprisingly quite luxurious; Pavlova, built for Marie Loftus, had many bedrooms, each done in a different colour, and a large dining room with 24 heavy oak chairs round a long table which in turn was adorned with valuable table silver. Many of the homes in Bungalow Town also contained pianos or organs. During the Second World War, Bungalow Town was destroyed to prevent it being used as a beach head. After the war it was rebuilt by the council and has become a tidy and respectable housing estate.

Shoreham Fort was a brick-built fortification believed to have been started in the Napoleonic era but not finished until 1857 and rendered obsolete in 1870 by developments in artillery. It was however still used for drills and parades until the end of the Victorian era, and guns remained in service there until 1921.

Now begins the long rather bitty negotiation of Shoreham Harbour (incorporating the Adur estuary) for a fair part of which you're forced to forsake the waterfront. Having got to the bank above the Adur, veer left; unfortunately you can't stick to the riverside so walk round past the fort, keeping it to your left, and walk through the fort car park to enter a road called Fort Haven. Follow this to a T-junction and turn right onto Harbour Road. You soon reach the conspicuously signed Quay Court and beside it there's a signed footpath which goes to the right of the buildings but soon returns to the road via a car park - hardly worth taking! However very shortly beyond that point, you can turn right onto Osprey Way which passes round the side of the modern housing development to arrive at the waterfront, and you can then follow an excellent waterfront walkway, keeping the splendid new houses and flats to your left. The views immediately across the estuary, part of Shoreham Harbour, aren't hugely inspiring, but the housing complex is undeniably impressive and tasteful. There's an inlet where you need to follow the walkway round, but you're soon back by the river and keep beside it till you're forced back to the road. Turn right to walk beside the road, then at the Waterside Inn bear right to rejoin the waterfront. On reaching the waterfront, veer left to follow the riverside briefly, soon arriving at and crossing the footbridge over the River Adur into the Shoreham town centre; known as the Dolphin Footbridge, it opened in 1921 to replace a ferry crossing. Having crossed the bridge you turn right onto the A259 to progress but you may want to stop and enjoy the town. The street leading to the town's superb church of St Mary is just here, a moment's walk from the footbridge, and along this street there were two excellent cafes at the time of writing.

Shoreham

New Shoreham is the closest port to London on the south coast of England. Historically, the Adur on which it stands was known as Bramber Water which at one time was deeper and wider than it is today, thereby enabling boats to navigate upstream to Steyning and Bramber. By the beginning of the 11th century, however, the silting of the estuary resulted in the port being moved nearer the river mouth, initially to Old Shoreham and then New Shoreham, planned and built as a "new" town by the Normans. Architecturally, only two real historical gems remain despite the long history of the town. The first is the **Church of St Mary de Haura** ("of the harbour") which dates back to 1130; despite losing its nave in 1720, it still boasts magnificent choirstalls and tower which at 81ft high is visible for miles. Some attractive flint-built cottages and walls are to be found near to the church. The second building of interest is the Marlipins, an unusual example of a surviving secular nonmilitary Norman building. Its exterior is made of very distinctive chequerboard flint and Caen stone;

once the customs house from which harbour administration was conducted, it later became a museum containing historic ship models and relics of local history.

New Shoreham was quickly to become famous, not architecturally but as a port. It was one of the leading ports of the medieval period, exporting wool, corn, salt and iron, and importing wine from France. It is further recorded that a large number of boats were engaged in fishing for mackerel and herring. The town also had an important association with shipbuilding, with reasonably-priced timber easily obtained from the Weald by being floated down the River Adur.

The port itself dwindled in importance the 16th century, but the fixing of the river mouth in 1818 and the opening of the eastern arm of the harbour in 1855 helped it to recover its prestige. A further development which boosted the port's fortunes was the laying of oyster beds within the river mouth, bringing prosperity to fishermen and carriers who made daily journeys to the capital with the freshly-caught delicacies.

The lighthouse at Shoreham which dates back to 1846

During one year in the 1850's, 20,000 tons were sent by rail from Shoreham. Strategically Shoreham was ideally placed to serve the rapidly-developing towns of Brighton and Hove, and over the 19th and into the 20th centuries, the port was handling timber from the Baltic, oil from the refineries at Fawley, Canvey and Milford Haven, gravel dredged from the English Channel, sand, coal, stone and...alcohol. In 1959 a bulk wine terminal was built at a cost of £400,000, and in the 1980's one fifth of Spain's sherry exports passed through the port. In the 1990's it was, controversially, handling live animal exports from this country, resulting in a number of angry protests from animal rights campaigners there in January 1995. By the end of the 20th century, Shoreham was handling 3 million tons of cargo per annum.

Historically Shoreham has, unlike Bognor, Worthing or, as we shall see, Hove and Brighton, always been more of a workaday place than a holiday resort, but it is a most pleasant town with fine views from the banks of the nearby River Adur back to Lancing College Chapel. The founder of the college Nathaniel Woodard, actually started a day school in the town with 24 pupils. Legend has it that pupils lived mainly on bread and cheese and "milestone pudding," so named because it was believed there was a mile between each currant contained within it!

Having joined the A259 from the footbridge, continue eastwards alongside this very busy road. It's a pretty grim slog past various retail and industrial units - although you may be glad of the McDonald's on your left! - but at length the road does reach the water's edge, passing the lifeboat station and lighthouse that dates back to 1846. There's a signed footpath and small area of beach beyond the lighthouse but it's not worth leaving the road to follow either. The river veers seawards here, but you keep water to your right, this being the start of a lengthy inlet forming the eastern arm of Shoreham Harbour and extending all the way to Hove. The result is another peninsula mirroring that of Shoreham Beach, which will delay your return to the open sea, but not for very long. Sticking to the A259 beyond the lighthouse there's some more rather dull pavement walking, but in a few hundred yards you pass the redbrick Shoreham Port Authority building opposite Grange Road; shortly beyond the Port Authority building turn right where indicated by a sign pointing you to the beach via the lock gates. The sign proclaims Brighton to be just 4 miles away.

Follow the walkway then in obedience to the arrow sign, bear right and then veer round to the left to access and cross the lock gates over Shoreham Harbour. Note, however, that the gates frequently open to let harbour traffic through, so don't be surprised if you have to wait. The locks and other developments you see hereabouts are all legacies of the huge reconstruction works that were undertaken in the port in the 1950's. Having crossed over it's a short walk to the seafront, with the huge funnel, an obvious landmark for miles around, close by to your left. Having reached the seafront, you have a choice: if you're in a hurry, turn left here (1) and strike out eastwards towards Brighton. However I do recommend you turn right and follow the seafront back to the mouth of the Adur and, if you're feeling energetic, continue along the harbour wall to its very end. You'll get a superb view to the Adur estuary, Shoreham and its surrounding countryside, and you'll be able to enjoy the crash of the waves against the wall. Then retrace your steps to point (1) and continue.

To begin with all is well: you have a pavement beside the beach with Basin Road South to your left, and behind that the eastern arm of Shoreham Harbour separating you from the sprawling communities of Southwick, Fishersgate and Portslade. As you pass along Basin Road South, you leave West Sussex and enter what used to be part of East Sussex but is now the discrete unitary authority area of Brighton & Hove. In due course, the road veers away from the shore and you lose the right-hand pavement. You could simply continue on the pavement, but it's dull going, and you may prefer to follow either the beach or, where it exists, a rough path at the top of the shingle bank. Be aware, however, that there are stretches where fencing separates the beach from the road, so don't think you can chop and change at will! You will reach a much firmer course along the top of the shingle bank; it is used by lorries, so be careful, but it's definitely preferable to the road.

At the far end of this course, by a mini-roundabout, you arrive at a section of private beach and are forced back to the road, continuing along it on the landward side of industrial units. This, at the far eastern end of Shoreham Harbour, is one of the less inspiring parts of your coastal walk! The road swings sharp left, and as it does, turn right onto a minor cul-de-sac to arrive at the start (or end) of Hove Western Esplanade. The worst is over and it's now plain sailing all the way to Brighton along a wide concrete promenade. Almost at once you pass Hove Lagoon, once a tidal reach of the Adur and now converted into a valued recreational facility, then walk parallel with Kingsway, here within striking distance of the centre of Hove. Perhaps the best entry into Hove's centre is by crossing Kingsway into Grand

Avenue, easily identified by its magnificent statue erected in honour of Queen Victoria's Diamond Jubilee.

Hove

Hove amounted to very little until the early part of the 19th century. It is recorded that during the reign of Henry V111, Hove consisted of nothing more than 12 houses and a church, and even three centuries later, in 1821, its population was just 300. By 1820, however, the westward development of Brighton had extended to the eastern boundary of the parish of Hove, and soon began to extend into the parish itself; in just 40 years from 1821 the population rose from 300 to 9000. Although the period between 1824 and 1840 saw very extensive building work in Hove, the quality of the building was extremely good, and during this period, the splendid **Brunswick Square** and **Brunswick Terrace** were developed, as well as the fine **Adelaide Crescent**, designed by Decimus Burton. Other buildings of merit dating from the 19th century were the **Avenues, Palmeira Square, Cliftonville, Denmark Villas, Osborne Villas** and **the Drive.** These properties encompassed a variety of Victorian building styles, some Regency style, some with distinctive yellow brick fronts and some Italianate, but all meriting conservation area status. In December 1882 the magnificent bold red brick Town Hall was opened, sadly burning down in January 1966, and 1890-91 saw the building of the superb **All Saints Parish Church** in 13th century French style in Eaton Road, built of Horsham sandstone.

Hand in hand with Hove's popularity as a place to live went popularity as a seaside resort, with parks, lawns and promenades growing up around the town, and a continuous esplanade was completed towards the end of the 19th century. The particularly impressive **King's Esplanade** was until 1909 named the Medina Esplanade and was completed in 1892. The locals loved the sea so much that seawater was stored in a reservoir and pumped into nearby houses so people could enjoy a seawater bath at home. In 1921 work started on developing the lagoon; once a tidal reach of the Adur, it was during the 1930's transformed into a delightful area of water, used for model yachting events and also as a training ground in the run-up to D-Day. Not surprisingly, Hove attracted a number of distinguished visitors, including the naturalist Richard Jefferies, the founder of the Salvation Army, General Booth, and Winston Churchill, who was educated at the Misses Thompson's Preparatory School at Hove between 1883 and 1885. During the 1890's, George Albert Smith and James Williamson began making films at Hove; they were among the earliest films ever made.

Fortunately, Hove came through both World Wars relatively unscathed, but today there are concerns that the erection of so many new houses and flats in Hove renders uneconomic the preservation of the area's fine terraces, squares and crescents, and deprives Hove of its special character. Perhaps, however, it will be a few years before it loses its nickname "Actually" after the supposedly snooty residents who if asked if they live in Brighton reply, "Hove, *actually!*"

Once you have passed Grand Avenue you are within easy reach of some of the best Regency streets in Hove, with Brunswick Terrace and Adelaide Crescent just across Kingsway. Once beyond Montpelier Road (B2122) leading north-east from the A259, you can be said to have left Hove behind and are now entering Brighton. Straddling the boundary is the Peace Memorial, dedicated to Edward VII and unveiled in October 1912. You pass the splendid Victorian bandstand, the remains of West Pier, the luxurious Grand Hotel, and the bland Brighton Centre, and can choose between two esplanades or the beach! As you get towards Brighton's unmissable Palace Pier, numerous roads leading off to the left provide access to Brighton's immense shopping centre with its many restaurants and cafes. The clearest and quickest access is by West Street (A2010).

Brighton

Brighton as we know it today did not start to develop until the latter part of the 18th century; there had been a town on the site on which Brighton stands, but this was virtually destroyed by fire in 1514. Towards the end of the 16th century it developed – as a herring fishing community, with 80 fishing boats in use, 400 mariners and 10,000 nets, although the fishing quarter has since been virtually swallowed by the sea. In those days, the place was known as "Brighthelmstone."

The undisputed founder of modern Brighton was Dr Richard Russell, who in 1750 was practising as a doctor in Lewes and sent patients to Brighton to try a seawater cure. He was one of a number of promoters of health to encourage people to Brighton;

Brighton's splendid Victorian bandstand

perhaps the most colourful entrepreneur in this field was an Indian, Sake Deen Mahomed, who established Mahomed's Warm, Cold and Vapour Baths. As a result of this concern for health, many notable people were drawn to Brighton towards the end of the 18th century, including Fanny Burney and Dr Johnson. In 1765 the Duke of Gloucester arrived, to be followed in September 1783 by his nephew the Prince of Wales, later the Prince Regent and King George IV; the royal doctor had apparently recommended sea bathing as a remedy for his swollen neck glands. Following the arrival of the Prince, many other upper-class visitors followed suit. Accordingly, efforts were made to erect larger houses and enhance older ones. In 1815 the Prince Regent appointed John Nash to build a palace to effectively replace the simple classical Marine Pavilion that Henry Holland had built some years before. The result was the remarkable Royal Pavilion which was completed in 1823 and which remains the most stunning building in Brighton, both inside and outside, the most notable rooms being the Music Room, the Great Kitchen and the Banqueting Room.

Besides the Pavilion, a huge number of buildings were erected in Brighton in the early years of the 19th century, and the town was thus blessed with a rich legacy of Regency architecture. The masterminds behind much of this were Charles Busby, Amon Wilds and his son Amon Henry Wilds. **Kemp Town,** so named because it was built for one Thomas Read Kemp, is regarded as the most outstanding architectural achievement of the partnership of Busby and Wilds senior, but many other buildings erected at this time are worthy of note, with good examples in **Silwood Place, Western Terrace, Oriental Place, Hanover Crescent, Montpellier Crescent, Belgrave Place, Powis Square, Bedford Square, Regency Square, Russell Square** and **Clifton Terrace.** Two of the most notable buildings to be constructed in Brighton during the 19th century included the **Grand Hotel,** designed in Italian Renaissance style and in 1864 regarded as the leading hotel of its day, and **St Bartholomew's Church,** then the biggest brick church in Europe, magnificently decorated with oil paintings and Italian mosaics.

1841 was a crucial year in Brighton's history, for it saw the arrival of the railway, and the consequent increase in holiday traffic served as a catalyst for the town's future development as a resort. The first pier to be erected in Brighton was the Suspension Chain Pier, constructed in 1823, although it was destroyed by a storm in 1896. The **West Pier** followed in 1866 and the **Palace Pier** in 1899; the Palace Pier, now effectively Brighton Pier, survives, but West Pier has been all but destroyed in recent years, with only a few sad remains out at sea. The Palace Pier was to become Brighton's most popular attraction and is still flourishing today. Two other significant attractions to arrive in Brighton in the 19th century were the aquarium, which opened in August 1872 and became an important entertainment centre, and **Volks Electric Railway.** This was named after its brainchild, Magnus Volk, the son of an immigrant German clockmaker. The railway was opened in 1883 with an extension to Rottingdean being built in 1896, although this extension lasted only four years. The extension was quite remarkable; the line actually followed along the beach which meant that at high tide the track was actually submerged by the water. The train was thus mounted on four stilts, and named "Daddy Long Legs!"

Although Brighton suffered severe damage in the Second World War, many wonderful unspoilt Regency streets remain, and the character and ambience of former times are preserved in its splendid shopping area of narrow streets known as **The Lanes.** Long before the impact of Dr Russell, those who did not depend on the sea for their livelihood had their homes on higher ground in a labyrinth of medieval streets, and it is this higher ground that the Lanes occupy today. The original buildings have gone, and the current ones date mainly from the 19th century, but they give a good idea of the atmosphere of the medieval town, and providing an oasis of antiquity in this very bustling resort.

Brighton today is unarguably the most vibrant centre on the Sussex coast. It is a shopaholic's paradise, with numerous streets across the town which are full of independent shops selling everything from Provencal tableware to lucky Buddhas, and restaurants catering for every taste. Now designated, with Hove, as a city and unitary authority independent of East Sussex (although most people think of Brighton as part of Sussex)it is now so cosmopolitan that it's known by some as "London by the Sea." It is noteworthy for its gay scene which dates back over 100 years, and gay icons such as Noel Coward and Ivor Novello have both spent part of their lives in the town. A number of celebrities have made Brighton their home including the boxer Chris Eubank, the disc jockey Norman Cook (alias Fatboy Slim) and the glamour model Katie Price. It hosts a major arts festival in the spring, its Theatre Royal hosts numerous prestigious productions attracting stars of international repute, and it is the final destination for the veteran car rally on the first Sunday in November as well as the popular London to Brighton Bike Ride in summer. A very recent attraction, which may tempt you as it is right on the seafront close to the pier, is the Brighton Wheel, almost identical to the London Eye in appearance; from the comfort of one of the pods you'll be able, on a clear day, to enjoy superb views of the Sussex coastline you've covered and still have to come. At the time of writing, though, it is uncertain how long the Wheel will stay in place, although it has planning permission to remain in situ until 2016. There are also plans for a splendid new tower close to the site of West Pier which will be Brighton's answer to Spinnaker Tower in Portsmouth and provide even better views to the surrounding coastline and countryside.

There's nothing subdued or shy about Brighton, and it will contrast markedly with the unspoilt coastal scenery you will meet elsewhere on your journey. But whether as a walker you decide you love Brighton or you hate it, you can be sure you won't easily forget it.

One of Brighton's newer visitor attractions and hopefully here to stay - the Brighton Wheel

SECTION 7 - **BRIGHTON TO SEAFORD**

SECTION 7 - BRIGHTON TO SEAFORD

Length:	12.5 miles.
Start:	Brighton Pier.
Finish:	Bottom end of Dane Road, Seaford.
Public Transport:	Regular buses serving Rottingdean, Saltdean, Peacehaven and Newhaven from Brighton; regular trains serving Seaford from Brighton.
Refreshments:	Rottingdean (P,C,S); Peacehaven (P,C,S); Newhaven (P,C,S); Seaford (P,C,S).
Conditions:	Although the walking in the Newhaven area is a little fiddly, this is on the whole very straightforward and easy going, with some sustained cliff walking for the first time on your coastal pilgrimage, and there is a great deal of variety with many interesting landmarks on or close to your route. If you are a strong walker you should be able to complete it in half a day. Public transport links are excellent, and you're never too far away from refreshment or supplies.

Beyond Brighton Pier, stick to the Esplanade, soon passing the splendid Brighton Wheel; not far beyond the Wheel you'll see the Volks Electric Railway starting up on your right, and you'll find the railway separating you from the shingle. However the sea is clearly visible so I suggest you stick to the concrete rather than joining the shingle. You pass the Half Way station, beyond which look out for and use one of the flights of steps to take you up to the raised promenade, Max Miller Walk; follow this raised promenade and go forward to climb a flight of steps where you join the coast road, Marine Parade. Follow the seaward side, getting splendid views to Brighton Marina below to your right, then more or less opposite Arundel Street, bear right to join a clifftop path. This is your first proper clifftop walking on the route, and in fact you'll be following the cliffs for the majority of the way to Newhaven. Looking down, you can see an undercliff path passing the back of Brighton Marina, but after so many miles of coastal walking I think you deserve a clifftop march! The views to the Marina, with its impressive waterfront houses and flats as well as boats and a number of businesses, are magnificent, as are the views to the sea beyond, and it's worth looking back for excellent views westwards to Brighton which you're now leaving behind. You pass the buildings of Roedean School, and a windmill; beyond the windmill you start to descend, and four miles or so from

Roedean School between Brighton and Rottingdean

Brighton, you arrive in Rottingdean. You need to veer to the right just before the White Horse pub which you see on the right at the bottom of the hill, but to detour to the village, continue briefly along the A259 and then turn left into the High Street.

Rottingdean

Originally a South Saxon settlement, it is thought its name means "The valley of the followers of Rota." Historically more important as an agricultural settlement than as a fishing community, it boasts some very attractive old buildings, including a number built from flint, brick and timber, and a charming green and pond. The flint **Church of St Margaret** is of Saxon foundation, and some pre-Norman Conquest work survives in the nave. The earliest complete secular building in the village is the Black Horse, which may date back as far as 1513, and which was a popular meeting place for smugglers. Rottingdean was well known as a smugglers' village, and in the late 18th century smuggling was rife, particularly in such commodities as tea, spirits, tobacco and lace. The smugglers found an unlikely ally in Dr Hooker, the vicar, who was so highly thought of by the smugglers' ringleaders that they invited him to lead a force of 50 men to repel Napoleon's invading hordes! With the rise in popularity of Brighton as a resort during the 19th century, Rottingdean too began to attract visitors during that time, drawn perhaps by its charming valley setting only a few miles from Brighton town centre, and its lovely old houses. Even today, despite so much development to the north of the village, it is still a most pleasant place to visit, with so many fine buildings, and good shops and restaurants. A number of very distinguished people stayed or lived here, including the Irish Unionist leader Edward Carson, the distinguished painter William Nicholson, the former chairman of Reuter news agency Roderick Jones, and Edward Burne-Jones, responsible for the glorious colouring and design of the windows in the chancel of the church. There are two buildings of particular interest which you will have passed on your way into the village. One is **Roedean,** the most famous of all girls' independent schools, which was founded by the Misses Lawrence in Brighton in 1885 and moved to its present site at the very end of the 19th century. The buildings, of Jacobean style, include a chapel dated 1906 and an art school and library that go back to 1911. The other is the 18th century **smock mill** with four sails; once used to store contraband goods, it owes its preservation to the fact that it has formed an important landmark to fishermen at sea. Arguably the most famous name to be associated with Rottingdean is Rudyard Kipling, who wrote some of his most famous work here, including *Kim*, his

Stalky stories, and his much-loved poem about Sussex with its reference to "our blunt bow-headed whale-backed Downs." Kipling was writing here when smuggling was still a comparatively recent memory, and was thus moved to pen his *Smugglers Song* with its famous line "And watch the wall, my darling, while the Gentlemen go by!"

As stated above, you need to turn right away from the A259 just short of the White Horse along a metalled walkway which brings you down to the undercliff path. Turn left to follow it. While the undercliff path was not the optimum route past Brighton Marina, it certainly is a much better option immediately beyond Rottingdean. It's lovely easy walking, albeit lacking the clifftop views, and you may feel somewhat

Viewed from above, Brighton Marina resembles a model village

vulnerable in particularly wet or windy weather, especially if the tide is very high at the same time; in those circumstances you may prefer to stick to the coast road (A259) from Rottingdean onwards. In any case, even assuming you have followed the undercliff path, you'll be forced to leave it at Saltdean, as the undercliff path is seen to peter out immediately ahead. Accordingly, when you reach a flight of steps, use them to return to the coast road and turn right alongside it, joining the cliff path which takes you uphill to a distinctive obelisk and weathervane. Sadly your clifftop walk is shortly interrupted; ahead of you you'll see a fence, and you'll find yourself forced landwards round the side of some works. You rejoin the roadside and follow it as far as the Smugglers Rest pub, but immediately before the pub you need to turn right onto a narrow (and, at the time of writing, unsigned) path which returns you to the cliffs. Veer left here to continue along the clifftops. It's now very easy and straightforward walking along the cliffs, mostly over grass; it is great to have the sea below you to your right, but not so great to have the residential sprawls of Telscombe Cliffs, Peacehaven and Peacehaven Heights to your left. The only real highlight is the George V memorial which signifies your passing the notoriously uninteresting and straggly town of Peacehaven. You can conveniently access the town centre from any one of the numerous roads leading away from the cliff to the left hereabouts.

Peacehaven

Perhaps the most amazing thing about Peacehaven is not the quality of its architecture, or lack of it, but the fact that it exists at all. It was the brainchild of the wealthy businessman Charles Neville who during the early years of the First World War saw this charming clifftop area as ripe for development. Work began in 1915 to build on the 650 clifftop acres that Neville had bought. Initially it was decided that the resort should be named New Anzac-on-Sea in honour of the Australians and New Zealanders who were stationed in the area at the start of the Great War and who took part in the hostilities. After the debacle at Gallipoli, however, it was felt that this name was insensitive and inappropriate, and Peacehaven was chosen instead, as a result of a national competition. A massive advertising campaign was launched to persuade people to buy a house in Peacehaven, while the grand opening of the Peacehaven Hotel on 29 September 1922 was marked by a military band, fireworks and bonfire. The only item of interest in the village, which fortunately is right on the route, is the **George V memorial;** erected on 30 May 1936, it bears a tribute to the recently deceased king, marks Peacehaven's position on the Greenwich meridian, and lists distances to all the outposts of the Empire. Once past this, however, you will set off again towards Newhaven with few regrets. Pevsner scathingly commented "What is one to say?" Peacehaven has been called a rash on the countryside. It is that, and there is no worse in England."

A foretaste of things to come - steep chalk cliffs between Brighton and Peacehaven near Saltdean

The coast path continues on beyond Peacehaven, the housing relents at last, and you're now able to enjoy a very fine cliff walk, with excellent views ahead to Newhaven and Seaford. Just take care not to stray too close to the cliff edge, and watch for one dip and slightly awkward crossing of a little stream using a bridge consisting of narrow metal strips. Generally, however, the going is easy and the surroundings much more unspoilt and rural, marred only by Newhaven Heights, a development of chalets, which come up very close to the clifftop, but your path steers a clear course between the houses and the cliff edge. Beyond the chalets, you continue along the path onto Castle Hill, aiming for a mast. Pass to the right of the mast and carry on along the clifftop, but 150 yards or so beyond the mast (there are couple of benches just on the far side of the mast) you reach an area of bushes, with a choice between a path going steeply downhill to the right or one veering left into the bushes. Pause and enjoy the superb views from here to the mouth of Newhaven Harbour. Don't be tempted to take the path veering right - it leads to sheer cliff faces which are obviously totally inaccessible - but take the path swinging left through the bushes; it arrives at a gravelled path onto which you turn right and which you follow downhill. Go forward to a metalled road which descends, veering left and then right to arrive at a T-junction with Fort Road(1). Your way is left, but you could detour as signed here to visit Newhaven Fort (see description of Newhaven below).

You've now reached the Ouse estuary and are forced inland to cross it, so follow Fort Road inland from (1) above, passing a boatyard which is to your right. Just beyond the boats, look out for a small parade of shops/businesses and turn right immediately before the first - at the time of writing it was named Haven Trading - to follow through the car parking area by the river, going forward into the metalled Riverside. You can now enjoy a pleasant waterside walk which has only comparatively recently become available to pedestrians; if you've worked up a thirst on your descent from your descent from Castle Hill, there's the handy Ark pub to your left. At

The George V Memorial, the only construction of any real interest in Peacehaven!

the top end of the riverside walk, bear right and go forward alongside the busy A259 to cross the swing bridge over the Ouse. This "opens" from time to time to allow boats through, so you may have a bit of a wait; opening times are usually advertised on local radio if you are anxious to plan your walk to avoid waiting. If you wish to explore Newhaven you will need to bear left having reached the A259 rather than turning right over the swing bridge.

Newhaven

Newhaven is not the prettiest town on your journey - Augustus Hare called it a "ugly, dirty-looking town and a smoky little port with dangerous drinking water!" but is a port of considerable importance, standing as it does close to the mouth of the Ouse. Although during Roman times the Ouse entered the sea where Newhaven is now, its course later turned towards Seaford, three miles further east, and the little settlement where Newhaven is now situated was known as Meeching. However in the late 16th century the river changed course yet again, to enter the sea at Meeching. Meeching was renamed Newhaven to denote a "new haven" growing up at the newly-formed river mouth, and it is as a harbour and port that the town was to become principally known. A harbour commission was formed in 1731 and by the middle of the 18th century ships of up to 150 tons were using the harbour. In June 1825 the General Steam Navigation Company advertised a fast sailing first-class steamer, the Eclipse, providing a service to Dieppe from the port every Tuesday and Saturday, weather permitting; the crossing, including a call at Brighton chain pier, took nine hours! During the 19th century the service improved greatly. In 1847 the Brighton and Continental Steam Packet Company was established with a view to starting a new cross-Channel service from Brighton. However, it proved to be unsuitable as a port,

Sheer cliffs at the eastern end of Peacehaven

with no harbour to protect the boats, and since the company was unable to come to terms with Shoreham Harbour Authority for a base there, Newhaven was chosen. The Newhaven-Dieppe service prospered from then on, and by 1891 the crossing time had been cut to 3 hours 45 minutes. During World War I civilian traffic across the Channel ceased and one of the cross-Channel steamers, the Paris, served as a minelayer. The port, used as a supply base during the First World War, was no less strategically significant during the Second, when it became a base for hospital ships, motor gunboats, minesweepers and air sea rescue missions. It was also the base for the disastrous Dieppe Raid in August 1942, with over 2700 of the 5000 soldiers who took part being killed or taken prisoner. After the war, the cross-Channel service for civilian traffic resumed, with a car ferry service being introduced in 1964. Newhaven remains the only port on the Sussex coast offering a year-round cross-Channel ferry service, but even that may be in jeopardy now as a result of the Channel Tunnel.

Despite its importance as a port - by 1880 it had become the sixth most important port in the country - the town never grew in the same way that Bognor, Worthing or Brighton did. It remains a pleasant place for the visitor; though it never developed as a holiday resort, it has in recent years boasted a yacht marina, and it maintains an intricate street pattern in its centre, as well as a steep High Street running up to its most interesting building, **St Michael's Church.** This contains a fine beamed roof, unusual interior decor with shades of blue and terracotta, some Norman features and a shingle spire, although Cooke describes the nave as "most appallingly utilitarian!" In the churchyard of St Michael's there is an obelisk dedicated to Captain James Hanson who, we are told, met his Maker "after a 4 year voyage of danger and difficulty round the world on discoveries with Captain Vancouver." Of perhaps greatest interest to the visitor is **Newhaven Fort** which you will have passed on your way from the Heights. The original brick-built fort was constructed in the 1860's during one of the periodic 19th century French invasion scares. It was equipped with modern guns during World War 2 and bombed several times by the Germans, but it has now been restored as a craft centre and museum. You can relive the days when it was an active fort with its gun emplacements, mortar batteries, magazines and parade ground. Cut into the steep cliffs, it is a fascinating area. There are some other good buildings including the **Bridge Hotel,** a white painted building which dates back to 1623. Louis Philippe, deposed in the 1848 uprising in France, stayed there after fleeing across the Channel, booking in with Queen Marie Amelie as "Mr and Mrs Smith."

The western mouth of Newhaven Harbour

Having crossed the swing bridge you fork immediately right onto Drove Road which goes over a level crossing beside Newhaven Town station; beyond the crossing you go first right into Railway Road, the road becoming Clifton Road and then Beach Road, but not getting any prettier. In fact this is certainly the dullest bit of the walk between Brighton and Seaford. As Beach Road bends sharply to the left by the railway, look for a footpath which leads off to the right, and you follow this path, staying parallel with (and to the land side of) the railway briefly then crossing the railway by means of a footbridge. Once over the bridge keep walking initially beside the railway but very shortly turn right over a bridge across Mill Creek to your right. Beyond the bridge bear left onto the signed path which follows the creek briefly then veers sharply right and, keeping buildings to the right, goes forward to a shingle bank with the beach beyond. Having reached the shingle, you could simply now turn left, south-eastwards, heading for Seaford which is clearly visible ahead, but I suggest before doing this you detour to the right and walk to the mouth of the Ouse. From here you get excellent views back to Castle Hill and the cliffs below it, and if you've time to spare you may want to walk to the end of the pier on the east side of the harbour mouth; it's a great place to watch boats coming in and out of the harbour. If you do this, however, please be very careful as there are gaps in the fencing giving sheer drops from the pier to the sea.

Now, whether you've made the detour or not, head south-eastwards towards Seaford, blessed with a choice between the beach and a metalled track running behind it. If the tide is out, the beach is better as you can walk to the water's edge where the going is much firmer, but when it covers these firmer areas the track is to be preferred. The track passes the site of the abandoned village of Tide Mills (see below). Beyond the sailing club building, which is very distinctive and easy to make out whichever route you take, there's a proper promenade known as the Bonningstedt Promenade. This passes the sprawling community of Bishopstone which is to the left, and goes forward to the buildings of Seaford, keeping Marine Parade to the left. As you arrive at the taller buildings immediately beside the seafront, and join the Esplanade, you reach the bottom of Dane Road and the end of this section; the centre of Seaford is reachable in a few minutes up Dane Road. This is a very good place to end your day's walk, as the next section is demanding!

Seaford

Back in the 13th century, Seaford was a busy port standing at the mouth of the Ouse, and in 1544 it was granted membership of the Cinque Ports Confederation. It had a proud tradition of fishing and shipbuilding, it imported wine from the Continent, and it exported wool from the flocks of Downland sheep. In 1342 it sent three ships to the Hundred Years War. The port began to go into decline owing to the activities of the sea, the relentless pressure of the waves shifting the shingle bank in such a way as to render the mouth of the Ouse virtually unnavigable. Towards the end of the 16th century the mouth of the river effectively transferred from Seaford to Meeching, providing the "New Haven" described above, and poor Seaford was left high and dry! For the next three centuries Seaford could be said to be in limbo, of no practical use as a port but yet to be developed as a resort. The townsfolk had to be constantly vigilant to the possibility of invasion by the French, with Seaford Bay regarded as a potential landing place. In 1545 an army led by Sir Nicholas Pelham, whose family was for years regarded as the town's aristocratic patrons, warded off the threat of French raiders here, just days after the French had sunk the Mary Rose. In honour of Sir Nicholas, the beach at the west end of the town was to become known as the Buckle, for it was a buckle which formed part of the coat of arms of the Pelham family. In 1806 the renewed threat of French invasion prompted the building of 74 **Martello Towers** along the south coast, the most westerly one being sited at Seaford, consisting of a gun platform, garrison and magazine. It was restored in the 1970's and is probably now the town's most interesting feature, housing a fine **museum.**

Once the threat of invasion receded, the town once more became something of a backwater. It was not until 1857, nearly a century after Dr Russell had begun the transformation of Brighton, that one Dr Tyler-Smith set up the Seaford Improvement Committee, thus inspiring afresh the possibility of a resort. The railway arrived in 1864 and the town's first sea wall was completed in 1865. Despite the lack of success of the endeavours of a number of companies to turn Seaford into another Brighton, many Victorians did enjoy visiting the town; its popularity as a watering place inspired the building of the fine Esplanade Hotel which survived for 80 years, attracting Edward VII for a stay in 1905. However it was obvious that there was only limited demand for another resort between Brighton and Eastbourne, and today one is left with the impression of a seaside resort which never quite happened. One curious phenomenon of Seaford in the early 20th century was the large number of schools - over 20 by the outbreak of World War 2 - and convalescent homes that were built in and around the town. Architecturally, there are a number of buildings of interest in Seaford. The most notable is arguably **St Leonard's Church,** described by Pevsner as a "large and monumental medieval church," of Norman origin and with a number of Norman features and unusual pillar carvings, although major restoration work was undertaken in the 19th century. There are many attractive houses as well. The **High Street** contains **No.2, Albion House,** built in 1714; **No.12,** which dates back to the mid 18th century; the early 19th century **Regency Restaurant;** and the mid-17th century **Old House.** Meanwhile, **Church Street** boasts the late 18th century **Alma House** and what was the **Tudor Town Hall,** although this is now much altered, and some 19th century buildings remain in the Steyne. Sadly, however, many of Seaford's old buildings have been pulled down to make way for uninspiring modern houses and shops, although some might consider the absence of the more garish and tacky trappings of a modern resort, such as amusement arcades and junk food bars, to be a definite plus for the town!

Tide Mills is a derelict village just over a mile north-west of Seaford; it consisted of a large tide mill and a number of workmen's cottages housing about a hundred workers. The mill stopped in around 1900 and the village was condemned as unfit for habitation in 1936, the last residents leaving in 1939. The area accommodated large numbers of Canadian troops during World War 2.

The Martello tower at Seaford is also a museum and is the first of many Martello towers you will see as you continue along the coast

SECTION 8 - **SEAFORD TO EASTBOURNE**

*Hope Gap with the mist-capped Seven Sisters
in the background*

SECTION 8 - SEAFORD TO EASTBOURNE

Length:	11 miles.
Start:	Bottom of Dane Road, Seaford.
Finish:	Bottom of Terminus Road, Eastbourne.
Public Transport:	Regular buses serving Cuckmere Haven on the Eastbourne-Seaford-Brighton route; regular trains serving Eastbourne on the Brighton-Hastings line.
Refreshments:	Cuckmere Haven (P,C); Birling Gap (C); Beachy Head (P); Eastbourne (P,C,S).
Conditions:	This is a superb walk, by far the best section of the entire route, with magnificent cliff scenery, the finest estuary in Sussex, and, to end, the loveliest resort in Sussex. Set a whole day aside for it and enjoy every minute!

You continue from Dane Road along the Seaford promenade. The front is dominated not so much by hotels and shops as residences, including the big modern redbrick Stratheden Court. The most interesting feature is the Martello Tower, now a local history museum, mentioned at the end of the previous section. You reach the end of the promenade at a car park, situated at the foot of the cliffs, and then begin the most strenuous cliff climb of the route so far, taking you to Seaford Head and its nature reserve. There is a choice of paths which maintain a clear course between the cliff edge on the right and the golf course on the left. The cliffs have been subjected to recent erosion, so keep back from the edge. The views from Seaford Head are tremendous, extending back to Brighton and beyond, and forward to the Seven Sisters and the Cuckmere valley. A clear track on springy turf now takes you forward across the cliffs.

Seaford Head

Seaford Head is the site of a triangular Iron Age hillfort. The area is known as "Buckle Church" - the Buckle being another reference, one supposes, to the Pelham family and its badge, referred to in the previous section, and the Church being a hermitage which is known to have existed here in 1372. Plants hereabouts include thrift, ground ivy and kidney vetch, and the area is also popular with rabbits.

Still enjoying superb views forward to the Seven Sisters, you now begin to descend on this excellent path, eventually arriving at Hope Gap. This is a quite delightfully secluded spot in a valley between rising cliffs; a detour down a flight of steps takes you to the rocky pavements separating the cliffs from the sea. To continue along the coast path you turn left at the foot of the slope, climbing to a more modest cliff top. Remaining on the cliff path, you approach the coastguard cottages. These used to be some considerable distance from the sea, but constant cliff erosion has brought them rather worryingly close to the cliff edge. Passing to the left of them you arrive at a clear track at right-angles to the cliff path you have been following. Turn right on to the track and descend, passing to the left of the houses, arriving at a gate. You have arrived at Cuckmere Haven, an area of flat land between cliffs at the mouth of the Cuckmere river.

Cuckmere Haven

The final passage of the Cuckmere river to the sea, between the cliffs of Seaford Head and the Seven Sisters, is marked by spectacular meanders. The mouth of the river has drifted east because of encroachments of the shingle beach, and in order to prevent flooding, a new cut was created in 1846, strengthened by automatic weir control. There was once a coastguard station on the way down from Seaford Head to

Looking back towards Seaford Head from above Hope Gap

Cuckmere Haven, with officers' quarters, flagstaff and boat house, all believed to have been built about the same time as the Martello Tower at Seaford. Although King Alfred is supposed to have founded a shipyard at Cuckmere Haven, the mouth of the Cuckmere is today one of the most unspoilt river mouths in the south-east of England, with no port complex, roads, caravan parks or any other modern trappings at all. It is the only river valley in Sussex to provide wildfowl with a natural merging of meadow marsh, saltings and a wild seashore. The coastline hereabouts has seen several shipwrecks, and at low tide it may be possible to see the remains of the German ship Polynesia, wrecked in 1890. The area was renowned in the 18th and 19th centuries as landing places for smuggled goods; a number of gangs operated from here, and there were some notorious encounters on the shore with customs officers. Some escapades were more successful than others. In 1923 an attempt was made to run a cargo of 91 cases of brandy aboard a French fishing boat from Dieppe, and at 9am on a Sunday morning the small craft left Dieppe intending to be met at Cuckmere. Unfortunately the pilot suffered sea sickness and after a most uncomfortable night was forced to land at Newhaven only to be met by the customs men!

Ignoring the arrow pointing left, pass straight through the gate and proceed on to the shingle beach, heading towards the cliffs on the other side of the beach. Your path is soon rudely

The Cuckmere Estuary, the most unspoilt estuary in Sussex

blocked by a channel of water. Do not, on any account, attempt to wade this channel, despite the fact that it looks so narrow and innocuous. There is no realistic possibility of fording it anywhere else, and annoying though it may seem, you are faced with a long trudge up to Exceat Bridge. When you reach the channel turn left to join a clear path which takes you along its west bank in an inland direction, the path moving slightly away from the channel just at the end. The walking is certainly very pleasant - though it could be muddy after heavy rain - with lovely views across the Cuckmere valley. When you finally reach the bridge crossing you are rewarded with the Golden Galleon pub! You walk through the pub car park then turn right to cross the bridge and continue alongside the busy A259. Fortunately a roadside footpath is available. The road bends sharply to the right and passes the interesting Exceat visitor centre there is a useful restaurant and tearoom here too.

Exceat

There was a little fishing village here in medieval times, but it was virtually wiped out by the Black Death in the 14th century. By 1460 just two dwellings of the original settlement had survived. Edward the Confessor, elected king in 1035, owned a manor at Exceat besides considerable other land in Sussex. The hamlet is not pronounced "Ex-seat" as one might suppose, but "Ex-sett" - despite being recorded as Essete in the Domesday Book!

More or less opposite the visitor centre, as the road bends left and begins to ascend, turn right into the car park, but almost immediately bear left through a gate along a path which goes forward to a metalled track. You now bear right onto this track and follow it back towards the sea, admiring the extraordinary meanders of the "old" Cuckmere estuary to your right. After roughly half a mile the path swings quite sharply left away from the valley, towards a group of farm buildings; don't swing left with it, but fork right onto a path signposted Seven Sisters, pass through a gate, then after about 100 yards fork left. You're now on the course of the South Downs Way. Initially your path remains on the flat but then proceeds up a flight of steps, going forward to a fence; don't cross the gate in the fence that soon appears, but keeping the fence to your right, press on uphill along a clearly marked path. This is quite a slog, but you can make it more enjoyable for yourself by pausing to look back at the superb views across Cuckmere Haven to Seaford Head. At length you arrive at the summit of the first of seven spectacular chalk clifftops known as the Seven Sisters. Take time to enjoy the amazing views to the Cuckmere valley and the downland beyond. Magnificent walking follows as you tackle the Seven Sisters in turn, sharp descents followed by stiff climbs. Descending from the final Sister, you pass through a gate and continue along a clear wide track, soon reaching a T-junction of paths; turn right to follow another wide stony track downhill. You pass the big car park, pub and café of Birling Gap, and at the bottom of the hill arrive at a road. Here you turn right and immediately right again into the car park, exiting from it almost at once by passing to the left of the telephone kiosk.

Seven Sisters and Birling Gap

The Seven Sisters, seven spectacular chalk cliffs, form the eastern end of the South Downs and the climax of the South Downs Way, and owe their origin to geological activity between 50 and 100 million years ago. Each clifftop or "sister" has a name: in turn they are Haven Brow, Short Brow, Rough Brow, Brass Point, Flagstaff Point, Bailey's Hill and Went Hill Brow. The depressions separating each "sister" are the valleys of ancient rivers, formed when the chalk extended further seawards, but later cut off when the sea pounded the chalk away. The unspoilt chalk hills attract many birds including the fulmar, wheatear and jackdaw, butterflies which include the blue butterfly, red admiral and clouded yellow, and such plant life as the cowslip, orchid, vipers bugloss and field fleawort; other plants which have been found here but are now seldom seen include round-headed rampion and carline thistle, as well as fungi such as lepiota and horse mushrooms.

Birling Gap, lying at the eastern end of the Seven Sisters, is a freak cleft in the South Downs with steep steps to the sea which were used by smugglers. Note the row of houses here and how exposed they are to the sea. The gap in the cliffs which exists here proved a godsend in November 1883 when a ship named the New Brunswick was seen in distress off the nearby Belle Tout lighthouse in a south-westerly gale, and it was decided to use the beach at Birling Gap as the launching place for the lifeboat. To get the lifeboat there it was necessary to pull it across the land, involving a 600ft climb over the hills.

Having passed the kiosk you begin climbing again, and you have a choice of paths to take you

Looking down towards Cuckmere Haven on the ascent to the Seven Sisters

up to and along the clifftops, aiming for the Belle Tout lighthouse. Note that you need to keep to the left of the lighthouse.

Belle Tout

The Belle Tout lighthouse was built from Aberdeen granite by Thomas Stevenson around 1830, and remained in use for the remainder of the 19th century. Unfortunately it proved somewhat ineffective in the thick mists which crept in from the English Channel and hung between the clifftop and the sea, curtaining off the beams which would then be invisible to shipping. As a result, it was decided to build a sea level light house to replace the Belle Tout lighthouse in 1902, and it is this lighthouse, below the Beachy Head clifftop, which remains in use to this day. The Belle Tout lighthouse became a dwelling but owing to cliff erosion has had to be moved more than once, and may have to be moved again. The area of downland around the present site of Belle Tout is of considerable archaeological interest; it was once an Iron Age camp and has been identified as a site of the ancient Beaker people. Plants to be found in the vicinity include the field fleawort, early purple orchid, early spider orchid and small hare's ear. During the 19th century poorer people ground up dried tubers of the early purple orchid and mixed it with hot milk, honey and spices to create salep, thought to have aphrodisiac properties!

You drop down steeply to meet the road at a small car park, then begin the assault on Beachy Head. It is a long, laborious climb, not helped by a big dip which sees you rapidly lose height which you must then of course regain, but the grass is lovely to walk on and the views just get better and better, with the tower blocks of Brighton clearly visible on a reasonable day. At length you reach the summit.

Beachy Head

The conquest of Beachy Head is arguably the most exhilarating and rewarding part of your Sussex coastal walk. At the summit, you are 535ft above the sea, and it is a frighteningly long and steep drop to the waters below. If you have a head for heights, make for the cliff edge (taking immense care) and look down at the 125ft high lighthouse, built to replace the ineffective one at Belle Tout at the beginning of the 20th century. The name Beachy Head is thought to derive from the Middle Ages French "beau chef," meaning "beautiful headland." It certainly is beautiful, offering views which on a clear day can extend back to the Isle of Wight and even across the sea to France; since 1990 it has once more become a breeding ground for falcons, and it is one of the best places in Sussex to see the stone curlew. However, it is also a dangerous place. The steep high cliffs have proved a fatal temptation for many wishing to take their own lives, while the seas below can be treacherous, and there have been numerous shipwrecks here. The headland has also seen hostilities in the form of the so-called Battle of Beachy Head in June 1690 between the allied English/Dutch fleets and a marauding French fleet. The biggest threat to Beachy Head is erosion, with a major cliff slip recorded in January 1999, and further slips cannot be ruled out.

When you arrive at the observation point a little before the summit, remain on the ridge and aim for the triangulation point, but just short of it, and just before you get level with the hilltop Beachy Head Restaurant, turn right on to a metal path. Shortly the metal path describes an extravagant loop, with a seat at its bottom end. Take the short cut across the loop using the path provided, but having done so, instead of turning left on to the metalled path again, go straight on over it to (very briefly) join a path that contours the hillside. Do not continue forward on this path, but turn right almost immediately to take a track which goes extremely steeply down the hillside. Take great care! From this track you can enjoy breathtaking views forward to Eastbourne and the coastline all the way to Hastings. Follow the wide track all the way to the cliff edge. On reaching it, turn left to follow the green clifftop path; it is lovely walking, with hills rising steeply to your left and the sea to your right. Ironically having lost so much height you must rise to meet a wide gravelled track, on to which you turn right. The track soon becomes a metalled road, now separated from the sea by housing. You drop down to a cafe marking the end of the South Downs Way and the beginning of Eastbourne. Beyond the café, turn right into Duke's Drive and follow it downhill. You pass the Helen Gardens, then immediately beyond these gardens you turn right along a road signposted Holywell, Promenade (Western Parade). Keep along this road, ignoring turnings off to the right, and you find yourself on the promenade. Turn left and enjoy an easy walk along the promenade into Eastbourne. In due course you have a choice of promenades: I suggest that you stick to

Looking towards Beachy Head and its lighthouse

the lower one, then, just beyond the bandstand, a little way short of the pier, climb onto the upper promenade beside the coast road. This section ends at the bottom of Terminus Road, which gives easy access to the town centre and the railway station.

Eastbourne

Eastbourne was just a small village until the mid 19th century. The village was inherited by William Cavendish, the 7th Duke of Devonshire, in 1834, and together with another local landowner, Carew Davis Gilbert, he set about developing it as a resort, with the main development beginning in 1851. By this time Brighton had already established itself as a popular seaside resort; the Duke deliberately set about creating something less extrovert and garish than Brighton, but still stylish and attractive with plenty of grand avenues, fine parks, gardens and greenery. The aim was for it to be the "Empress of Watering Places," and even today the town's three-mile esplanade and three-tier promenade, with its mix of private villas, handsome hotels, landscaped gardens and banks of flowers, remains relatively uncluttered by the traditional trappings of the modern resort.

There are a number of fine old buildings in Eastbourne. Some of the best are in the old town, situated about a mile inland; they include the flint and stone **Church of St Mary** in Church Street, with several Norman features, the fine timber-framed **Lamb Inn,** the flint 16th century **Old Parsonage** and 18th century **Manor House** which latterly has housed the **Towner Art Gallery** and **Local History Museum.** Other buildings of interest in the town include the 19th century **Church of St Saviour** in South Street; the 1884 **Town Hall** of brick and Portland stone, containing a tall tower and domed cap; the **Devonshire Park Theatre** of the same year with two identical Italianate towers; the magnificent **Grand Parade,** being the one terrace in the town Pevsner thinks stands comparison with the best architecture of Brighton; the mid-19th century bow-fronted houses of **Cavendish Place;** the extremely impressive late 19th century **Cavendish Hotel;** and the early Victorian Italianate houses of Trinity Street. The combination of greenery and fine architecture attracted some notable personalities including Charles Darwin, who wrote part of his *Origin of species* in one of the houses on Marine Parade, and the French composer Claude Debussy who stayed here for a while in 1905 and wrote part of his famous "La Mer" during his stay. The well-known writers Rumer Godden and Angela Carter were both born in Eastbourne, while Dr John Bodkin Adams went on trial in 1957, accused (and subsequently found not guilty) of the murder of a number of patients of his practice in the town.

Despite the fact that the town is primarily a holiday resort, it has been an important base for sea rescue and sea defence. Not only has the town's lifeboat been called out on numerous occasions, but Eastbourne also played an important part in coastal defence against the threat of Napoleonic invasion. To combat this menace, a massive brick building in Royal Parade known as the Redoubt was constructed in the town in 1803 to supplement the Martello towers. In modern times it has become the Sussex

Combined Services Museum, featuring a history of the Royal Sussex Regiment which was founded in 1701.

The town remained a prosperous resort well into the 20th century, but it was badly bombed during World War 2. However despite rapid post-war development which rather spoilt its Victorian charm, visitors have continued to be drawn not only to the lovely sands and excellent bathing, but to such features as the stunning Carpet Gardens, established in the town for more than a century; Devonshire Park with its tennis courts which play host to an important international women's tennis tournament in the run-up to Wimbledon in each year; the Towner Gallery with its impressive collection of contemporary art; the county cricket ground known as the Saffrons; the pier with concert hall and pavilion, completed by Eugenius Birch in 1872; a bandstand which was built to accommodate over 3000 spectators; and numerous tourist attractions which include the military museum referred to above, and the How We Lived Then Museum Of Shops in Cornfield Terrace giving a glimpse of what shopping was like in days gone by, containing over 75,000 exhibits. Eastbourne's summer seafront air show, known as "Airbourne," is now a major event, drawing huge crowds.

Midway over the Seven Sisters

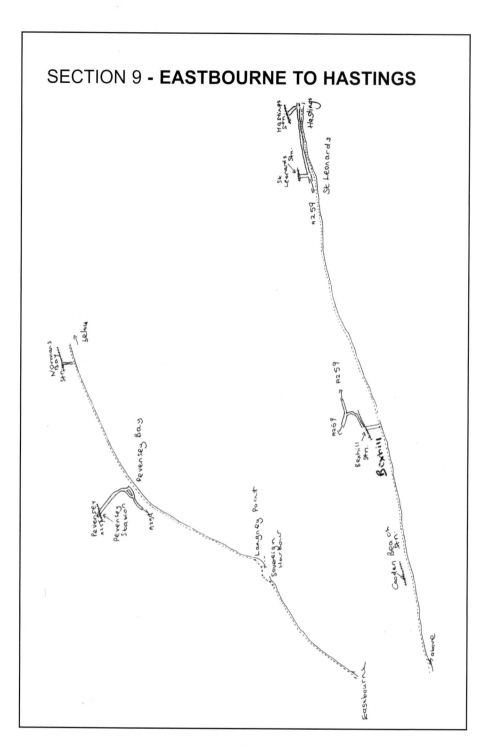

SECTION 9 - EASTBOURNE TO HASTINGS

Length:	14 miles.
Start:	Bottom of Terminus Road, Eastbourne.
Finish:	Bottom of Albert Road, Hastings.
Public Transport:	Regular trains serving Pevensey & Westham, Pevensey Bay, Normans Bay, Cooden Beach, Bexhill, St Leonard's Warrior Square and Hastings on the Eastbourne-Hastings line.
Refreshments:	Pevensey Bay (P,S); Bexhill (P,C,S); St Leonard's(P,C,S); Hastings (P,C,S).
Conditions:	This will inevitably feel rather tame after the exciting walking of the previous section; there is only a negligible amount of cliff walking, and at high tide there is a sustained piece of shingle tramping which will test your resolve quite considerably. However there are a number of highlights, including the splendid Sovereign Harbour complex, the historic village of Pevensey (via a detour), the pleasant town of Bexhill, the excellent views from the clifftops between Bexhill and Hastings, and the variety of attractions in Hastings itself. The second half of the walk is undoubtedly much easier than the first.

Beyond Terminus Road, continue along the Eastbourne promenade, passing the pier then reverting to the "lower" prom to continue. It's worth looking back from time to time, in order to enjoy splendid views back to Beachy Head and also to appreciate the variety of buildings around you including opulent hotels, the flint-fronted Ye Olde Bakery, dated 1790, and the Redoubt Fortress (see the description of Eastbourne at the end of Section 8). There's a little kink to the left and then right, but the going is quick and easy all the way to an area of boats and associated buildings which separate the concrete walkway from the sea. You may wish to join the shingle here to enjoy an uninterrupted view to the sea, secure in the knowledge that soon the walkway again becomes within sight of the water, and when it does so, you can simply rejoin it and proceed. Note that the walkway also doubles as a cycleway and you need to watch and listen for cyclists! Now pulling away from Eastbourne itself - but continuing to take the odd glimpse back towards the town and Beachy Head behind it - you pass the huge Sovereign Leisure Centre and adjacent amusement park. Your walkway is built on shingle that has been thrown up by the seas, with sea kale, yellow-horned poppy and sea campion all to be found nearby.

You pass the large redbrick water treatment works, then go forward to within clear sight of a Martello tower, where rather abruptly your trusty walkway stops. Don't bear left as signed here, but go straight ahead over an area of shingle, aiming straight for the tower. Immediately ahead of you here is Langney Point and the mouth of Sovereign Harbour; this is your only natural obstruction on this section but thankfully not requiring as lengthy an inland detour as the Ouse or Cuckmere estuaries have demanded of you! As you reach the Martello tower, turn left and cross rough shingly ground to pick up an excellent harbour-side path, now entering the modern and hugely impressive Sovereign Harbour complex. When the first edition of this book appeared in 2002, the complex was very much in its infancy, and construction work was still in progress, but now the way through is clear. You arrive at two pairs of swing bridges providing entrances and exits for boats entering and leaving the harbour. Simply choose whichever ones happen to be open in order to negotiate the harbour waters, then, before proceeding, pause to enjoy the variety of modern architecture on show, as well as the splendid range of vessels. Having crossed, aim for and pass to the right of the lifeboat station and

continue along the waterfront, veering right to arrive back at the beach, now on the east side of the harbour. You then swing left to follow an excellent concrete walkway at the back of the beach, with modern housing alongside you on the landward side. At the end of the modern housing, you veer to the right to get onto the beach side of the houses making up the bottom end of Pevensey Bay. You should be able to see the magnificent ruins of Pevensey Castle from here.

Looking towards Langney Point from Sovereign Harbour

Now the character of the walk changes completely as you face some 3 miles of pathless beach walking all the way to Cooden Beach, past the architecturally uninteresting sprawls of Pevensey Bay and Normans' Bay. If you are lucky, the tide will be out and you can proceed along the sands, only leaving them at the fine mock Tudor house at point (1) below; the only irritant is the large number of breakwaters which may turn the walk into a bit of an obstacle course unless the tide is low enough for you to sidestep them altogether. However if the tide is too high, you will have no choice but to follow the shingle. There are limited opportunities for relief; that said, a car park close to the beach just over a mile from the start of your shingle tramp does provides easy access to the amenities of Pevensey Bay. From the car park it is a straightforward detour (about another mile) to the historic village of Pevensey via Sea Road and the A259 Wallsend Road. It is certainly worth the detour and it'll make a welcome break from the shingle.

Two views of Sovereign Harbour, a very recent and very impressive waterfront development just east of Eastbourne

Pevensey

Pevensey is a most interesting place and well worth the detour inland. It once stood on a peninsula jutting into a large harbour protected from the sea by shingle spits. Subsequently the harbour silted up, the waters of the Channel have receded, and land reclamation has left the village nearly two miles inland, surrounded by marshland known as the Pevensey Levels. In the third century AD the Romans built their great defensive fortress of Anderida here; after they left, it was occupied in turn by the British, the South Saxons and King Alfred. It was taken over by the Normans when they invaded here from France on 28 September 1066. In recognition of its strategic importance, and to impress the native population, a new stronghold, **Pevensey Castle,** was built inside the **Roman walls** (which are still visible today) and the fort continued to be garrisoned until the 14th century. The castle was re-fortified during the Spanish Armada and again during the Second World War. In the Plantaganet era Pevensey became one of the Cinque Ports, and it developed as a port during the Tudor period; one of the port's most significant exports was iron from the foundries of the northern Weald. However, silting caused the port to go into terminal decline and by the end of the 16th century there were no mariners or fishermen left.

Among many splendid old buildings in Pevensey are the Early English **Church of St Nicholas,** east of the castle, and the half-timbered **Old Mint House,** dating from approximately 1342, although a mint was on this site from 1076; it was turned into an antiques centre, but its beautifully panelled rooms were once used by smugglers. Despite its comparatively small size, Pevensey was a bustling commercial centre, retaining a mayor and corporation until 1883, and also a Town Hall which is claimed to be the smallest in England. Justice was dispensed in this building, hence its also being known as the Court House. On one occasion a man appeared in court charged with theft of buckskin breeches, then a capital offence. In order to avoid sentencing him to death, the jury found him guilty of manslaughter! Subsequently the Court House became a museum, with exhibits which include the original magistrates' benches and the fossilised footprints of a dinosaur.

Beyond the car park at Pevensey Bay it will be very tough going indeed unless you're able to get down onto the sands and are able to dodge or surmount the breakwaters. In places your shingle tramp, if that indeed is forced on you by the tide, will be mitigated by the fact that excavators, extracting sand and shingle from the beach, have flattened the stones and created quite a reasonable surface. When I walked this section in February 2012, considerable excavation work was in progress, apparently for the purpose of strengthening sea defences, and further construction work, creating obstacles and "no-go" areas on the beach, can't be ruled out. Relief is temporarily available in the form of a narrow concrete ledge within sight of Normans' Bay station, and not far beyond Normans' Bay, as the railway gets closer to the beach, you can walk along the metalled Herbrand Walk parallel with the railway. However that veers away from the shore and you're faced with further and quite arduous shingle tramping as you pass the houses of Cooden Beach. At length you reach a splendid mock-Tudor house and garden backing on to the shingle (1) and very shortly beyond the house a metalled promenade begins. Now it's plain sailing all the way to Bexhill and in fact you'll be walking on concrete almost all the way to Hastings. Follow the promenade which duly peters out, but it's only a short shingle walk from here to a nearby toilet block where you pick up another and wider promenade which takes you on to Bexhill.

Bexhill

The old town of Bexhill was built half a mile inland from the sea and remains the most historic part of today's Bexhill, with an old, possibly 14th century, **Manor House** believed to have been built for the Bishop of Chichester; attractive brick and weatherboarded houses round the **Church of St Peter;** and a fine Georgian house at the end of Church Street more or less opposite the Manor House. The church's original foundation dates back to 772 when King Offa declared its site a "holy hill" and paid for a church to be built. The present church, standing on a Neolithic earthwork, was built in Norman times, and contains a tower that dates back to 1070, but its most famous relic is the so-called **Bexhill Stone,** a sandstone slab of 8th century origin, thought to be the lid of a reliquary containing the bones of a saint. The church has been very heavily restored, but considerable Norman work remains. The town was developed as a resort by the Earls De La Warr, who owned the land between old Bexhill and the sea, in the 1880's. It enjoyed many royal visits, and in 1901 it became the first resort in the country to permit mixed bathing. In May 1902 it hosted the first international motor-racing meeting on British soil, attracting many fine vehicles from the Continent.

Despite the fact that Bexhill was never to achieve the predominance as a resort enjoyed by its neighbours Eastbourne and Hastings, the needs of visitors were certainly not neglected. 1896 saw the opening of the Kursaal centre, offering traditional pier type entertainment (the resort was never to acquire a pier) but this later closed and was subsequently occupied by the town's Sailing Club. Effectively it was superseded by the huge **De La Warr Pavilion,** designed by German architects Erich Mendlesohn and Serge Chermayeff and built in the 1930's (although it looks a lot newer) and whilst under construction was nicknamed "King Kong's Meccano Museum!" To this day it is the focal point of the resort with ballroom, concert hall and theatre, and offers a wide range of entertainment and events for

The remarkable De la Warr Pavilion at Bexhill; it's hard to believe it was built as long ago as the 1930's

everyone from theatre goer to collector. Other attractions in the resort include the town museum, the terraced **Manor Gardens** and the splendid **Museum of Costume and Social History.** Nowadays Bexhill has become a largely residential and retirement town, and indeed more than half of its population are retired people. Two famous names to be associated with Bexhill are the author Angus Wilson who was born here, and the comedian Eddie Izzard who was brought up in the town.

Atop one of the two small pieces of cliff between Bexhill and Hastings

Follow the promenade past the very prominent clock tower, crazy golf course and De La Warr Pavilion; you turn sharp left into Channel View but then turn right almost immediately to continue along the promenade, passing the Sailing Club and a green with a stone marking the finishing line of the 1902 motor-racing meeting. The promenade ends at the Bexhill Sea Angling Club and you have a choice between a bracing walk over the cliff which lies straight ahead, using a good concrete walkway, or following an equally good concrete path across the shingle under the cliff. To gain access to the latter, fork to the right of the treatment works. The concrete undercliff path peters out beyond the cliff, so scramble over the shingle to join the concrete walkway, the railway separating you from a sprawling retail park. Once past a cafe, you again have a choice: a cliff walk, with a choice of paths, or a good path across the back of the beach, both meeting up once the cliff is passed. Now things are very straightforward, as you press towards the massive built up area of St Leonards and Hastings past Glyne Gap and Bulverhythe, following a good firm path along the back of the shingle beach, with the railway running immediately to your left. At length you pass a line of beach huts and reach a T-junction of paths with a fence immediately behind. Turn right at this T-junction, pass to the left side of a barrier and join a metalled road which brings you to a small parking area. Cross this area and briefly get on to the shingle, proceeding past a row of chalets with private forecourts. Just beyond this row of chalets there are some white railings, and by turning left here and climbing a couple of steps you gain access to the metalled promenade which will take you all the way to Hastings. Just like the Hove-Brighton promenade it begins somewhat tentatively, passing the undistinguished shops and flats on the edge of St Leonards, but it then widens, giving fine views to Hastings Pier. The Royal Victoria Hotel on the seafront adjacent to Marine Court effectively marks the centre of St Leonards.

St Leonards

St Leonards, named after the saint to whom its original church was dedicated, is, like Hove, the genteel western extension of a large seaside town. In fact it was designed as a completely separate development from Hastings by the architect James Burton, father of Decimus who designed the Hyde Park Corner screen. He bought an estate here and in 1828 started building a new resort on which to create a watering-place similar to Brighton. He actually put forward a scheme for a small harbour costing £6000 in 1831 but failed to find sufficient investors. It is clear that in his work in St Leonards, Burton was inspired by his illustrious son. The centrepiece was the fine stuccoed brick building which was to become known as the Royal Victoria Hotel, and this is arguably the finest building in the resort, with its splendid columns. Among other excellent work by Burton in the resort was an elegant group of Regency villas on either side of the impressive landscaped **St Leonards Gardens,** built on the site of a quarry. Rider Haggard, author of *King Solomon's Mines,* lived at the castellated **North Lodge** at the top of the gardens. Tudor and Gothic styles are well represented around the gardens; look out for the Gothic-style **Clock House** and for **Quarry Hill** and **Maze Hill,** detached villas inspired by Decimus Burton's work in Regent's Park. Two other buildings in St Leonards are worthy of mention. Firstly there is Burton's **Masonic Hall,** the southern side of which is based on a Greek Doric temple. Secondly, and immediately adjacent to the Royal Victoria Hotel, is the huge Marine Court complex, designed in the 1930's to look like an ocean-going liner, and built in 1937/38. To quote Pevsner, "With this block, the Copacabana got hold of the enterprising developers, and they have not let go since.... (It was) the first modernistic affront to the English seaside."

Love it or loathe it? Marine Court at St Leonards, built to resemble an ocean liner

Beyond the Royal Victoria and the Marine Court complex you go past the *verdant Warrior Square, consisting of a formal garden laid out in 1853 and regarded as the meeting point of St Leonards and Hastings. From Warrior Square, continue on towards Hastings pier; in due course you have a choice between the upper promenade, a lower promenade which is under cover for much of its length approaching the pier (handy if it happens to be raining), or indeed the beach! Whichever route you take, continue on along the waterfront past the pier and the fine White Rock Pavilion opposite, then beyond them I suggest you stick to the pavement by the coast road, looking out for the Albert Road turning off to the left. A pedestrian crossing provides safe and convenient access to this road from the seaward side of the coast road. This section ends at this point; by walking down Albert Road you immediately arrive in the very centre of modern Hastings, veering shortly left to reach the principal shopping area. The railway station is just a short way from here via Havelock Road.*

Hastings

Founded by the Saxons, Hastings was one of the original Cinque Ports together with Dover, Hythe, Romney and Sandwich, and was already an important harbour town at the time of the Norman invasion. During the Middle Ages it regularly contributed ships to the Navy. Although its importance as a naval town declined, it continued to be a bustling fishing port. The old town grew up in the valley between two sandstone ridges, East Hill and West Hill, and although the old harbour has long since been destroyed by the ravages of nature, there remain a host of historic buildings as evidence of the town's long and colourful history. There are even ruins of the **Norman castle** still to be seen on West Hill; it was built by Robert Count of Eu shortly after 1069, and the keep was built by Henry II in 1172. Most of the castle has now been washed away by the sea. From West Hill, narrow lanes lead steeply down to the old centre. The historian may well wish to make a beeline for the two historic churches, the only ones left out of Hastings' original seven medieval churches. The Perpendicular **All Saints' Church** dates back to the early 15th century and contains a particularly striking wall-painting depicting Christ in judgment. **St Clement's Church** was rebuilt in about 1390 having been destroyed by the French during one of their many raids in the course of the Hundred Years War, and following further skirmishes with the French at the end of the 17th century, a cannonball became lodged in the church tower.

There are many other buildings of historic interest in the old town, and a whole day could be spent pottering around the numerous streets and alleys, many extremely steep, from Tackleway at the eastern end of the old town with its impressive 18th century **East Hill House,** to **Exmouth Place** at the western end, the home of Elizabeth Blackwell, the first woman in the world to qualify as a doctor. The very names of the streets - **Tackleway, Rock-a-Nore Road, Winding Street** (which contains the scanty remains of the 14th century **sea wall)** - invite exploration. However the focal point of your wanderings should be the **High Street**. Particularly worth seeing here are **Torfield** and **Old Hastings House,** both dating back to the mid 18th century, the Georgian grey-brick **Wellington House,** and the Georgian-fronted **Apothecary House,** next to which is a house where Dante Gabriel Rossetti lived in 1854. The High Street also contains many old half-timbered houses. Off the High Street are many narrow alleys or twittens, one of the prettiest being **St Clement's Passage** leading to the church of that name, while All Saints' Street, running parallel with the High Street, also boasts many buildings of interest including the timber framed **Shovells,** home of a 17th century admiral, and a number of fishermen's cottages. Fishermen, traditionally dressed in thigh-length leather boots, long oilskins and sou'westers, have always played an important part in Hastings life. The importance of Hastings' thriving fishing industry is reflected in the **Fishermen's Museum** - once the church of the fishing community - on the seafront in Rock-a-Nore Road, near to the tall black-tarred wooden huts or "net shops" where fishermen would store their gear and hang out their nets to dry. There are also displays devoted to the fishing industry in the **Old Town Hall Museum** on the

High Street. Opposite the Fishermen's Museum is the **Mermaid,** once the headquarters of the Winkle Club, a charitable organisation requiring its members to carry a winkle in their pockets at all times on pain of payment of a fine!

Though visitors started to arrive from about 1775 onwards, Hastings was only really developed as a resort in the 1820's, with squares and terraces of seaside houses, many Regency in style, being built to the west of the old town. James and Decimus Burton, together with one Joseph Kay, were responsible for much of the design. Perhaps the finest street is the Regency **Pelham Crescent,** developed in the 1820's by the 1st Earl of Chichester with its 1828 **Church of St Mary in the Castle;** the church got its name because it is the replacement of the church in Hastings Castle, and its conception derives from the Pantheon. Also of note is **Wellington Square,** which again dates back to the 1820's and lies close to the castle ruins. Visitors' needs were catered for by the Italianate **Queen's Hotel,** dating back to 1858, and the **Palace Hotel** (later **Palace Chambers)** with its mixture of Renaissance and Baroque motifs, built in 1886. The pier was built in 1872 but as recently as October 2010 it was very badly damaged by fire; at the time of writing (March 2012) it remains a sorry sight, although it is hoped that it might be restored rather than abandoned to the ravages of nature. The White Rock Pavilion beside the pier was completed in the 1920's.

The town, although enjoying considerable popularity with holidaymakers during the 19th century and still attracting many visitors today, possesses neither Brighton's charisma and youthful exuberance, nor Eastbourne's elegance. It remains a bustling workaday place, with industries that have latterly included not only fishing but engineering and the manufacture of scientific instruments and domestic appliances, but it has more than its

Looking down on Hastings from just below East Hill

fair share of social problems, with - in 2005 - the second highest divorce rate in the UK; it is described by Brewer's Britain and Ireland as "one of the social blackspots of southeast England." Well-known personalities associated with Hastings include John Logie Baird who did much of his research into the formation of television here, and Sophia Jex-Blake, the women's rights campaigner who was born in the town.

SECTION 10 - **HASTINGS TO BROOMHILL SANDS**

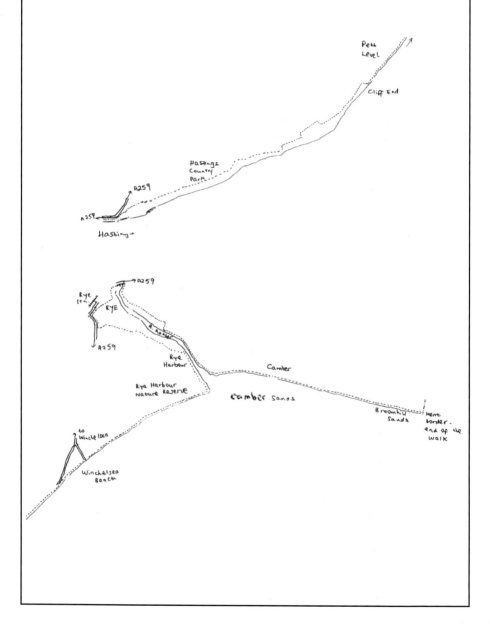

SECTION 10 - **HASTINGS TO BROOMHILL SANDS**

Length:	16 miles (add 1 further mile for return to Camber from Jury's Gap).
Start:	Hastings seafront, junction of Albert Road with A259.
Finish:	Jury's Gap.
Public transport:	Regular trains serving Rye on the Ashford-Brighton line; regular buses serving Camber on the Lydd-Rye-Hastings route.
Refreshments:	Pett (P,C); Winchelsea Beach (P,C,S); Rye Harbour (P); Rye (P, C,S); Camber (P,S).
Conditions:	This is a long but superbly rewarding concluding section with perhaps the greatest variety of any section in this book. You will enjoy cliff walking, some beach strolling and some really delightful riverside scenery, and you will pass right through Rye, one of the most beautiful towns in Sussex. You will certainly be finishing on a high note. It is a long day's walk and will need at least a day to complete it; indeed you may want to spend two days doing it, incorporating a stay in Rye.

NOTE: The very last half-mile of this final section will be inaccessible when firing is taking place on the Lydd Ranges. Firing takes place most days including weekends. To avoid disappointment I suggest you go online or telephone in advance to check non-firing days and times.

From the pedestrian crossing of the A259 coast road at its junction with Albert Road, the end of the previous section, continue along the seafront using the cycle track/walkway provided. All too soon, however, the walkway is forced to veer to the left, separated from the seafront by a large amusement park. Keeping the amusement park to the right with the coast road to the left, continue along the footway to the point where the A259 veers sharply left at its junction with Rock-a-Nore Road. Go straight on into Rock-a-Nore road but very shortly turn left up All Saints Street and, immediately before the redbrick Crown Inn, right into Crown Lane. You rise steeply to a T-junction with Tackleway at the top, and go straight over, up a flight of steps onto East Hill. Before climbing the steps, it's worth detouring briefly right at the T-junction and walking to the dead end from which there's an excellent view down to the black wooden fishermen's huts. Whether you've done the detour or not, you then do need to climb the steps as indicated above in order to proceed. It's quite a stiff climb but your reward is your arrival on East Hill, the site of an Iron Age hillfort, and now a pleasant green. Very soon after arriving on East Hill you reach an information board and a signpost with an arrow pointing right to Firehills; you will be following signs to Firehills for some miles! Observing this one, bear right to follow the right-hand side of the green, close to the cliff-edge fence, and go forward to a proper path. You are now in Hastings Country Park.

Hastings Country Park

Between Hastings and Fairlight Cove lie 5 miles of magnificent unspoilt countryside including deep wooded glens, heather clad hills and fine sandstone cliffs consisting of some of the oldest rocks in the South East. Over 540 acres were formed into the so-called Hastings Country Park in 1974; much of the park has been designated a Site of Special Scientific Interest.

Towards Ecclesbourne Glen on the dramatic cliff walk from Hastings to Firehills

The next four miles or so are scenically the best of this section. In summary they consist of three spectacular descents to wooded glens followed by stiff climbs, but the views throughout are quite majestic; veterans of the South West Coast Path may perhaps for the only time on their Sussex coast pilgrimage be reminded of the precipitous cliff paths of Devon and Cornwall. Keeping the cliff-edge fence to your right you begin your first descent into Ecclesbourne Glen, a wooded valley that 200 years ago was popular with smugglers and which provides ideal nesting territory for tits and warblers. Ensure you continue to observe the Firehills signs! Steps aid your descent, and after the crossing of the very narrow stream at the narrow valley bottom, you use steps to rise from the glen. For a while the going is less strenuous, but then again you find yourself descending to Fairlight Glen, ensuring that as you descend you fork right as indicated (again observing the Firehills sign). This glen is arguably the loveliest of the trio, with beautiful woodland on your descent, carpeted in spring with bluebells and wood anemones, while at the valley bottom a stream runs between large boulders under the trees. Then up you rise again. Don't be alarmed that on your ascent the path veers left away from the sea; shortly you reach a signed junction, bearing right and, after a brief level spell, you begin to descend (a path provides a detour to the cliff edge with glorious views, but it is a dead end so you'll need to go back). Now descend to the final glen, Warren Glen, less thickly wooded than the previous two but still populated with oak, hazel, beech and ash. A signpost in Warren Glen shows a path detouring off to a Visitor Centre in the village of Fairlight which boasts a church with an impressive hilltop setting; that said, it's a fair detour and with many miles still to do you may prefer to press on. However your coast path climbs

More like Devon or Cornwall than Sussex -
a superb view back from above Warren Glen

yet again, and you have another stiff ascent to the hilltop area known as Firehills, watching and listening for the yellowhammer or stonechat and enjoying yet more majestic views. There's a superbly sited bench, inscribed to "Sue" where you may wish to sit and rest and admire the scene, and thank the benefactors for their thoughtfulness. Beyond the bench you arrive at an area of green, within shouting distance of a mast, but instead of going up to the mast you now veer right to enjoy a fantastic cliff-edge path, maintaining height.

Sadly this doesn't last. In due course the path ends, and you go forward to a narrow path between fences and then a wide stony track, descending gently, keeping the houses of Fairlight Cove to your left. You arrive at a junction with Shepherds Way, and at this point you have to leave the cliffs, the result of subsidence which is a major problem over the next mile, and embark on a rather

uninspiring walk through Fairlight Cove. Observing the footpath sign, turn left along Shepherds Way then shortly right into Bramble Way; you go over a crossroads with Smugglers Way and forward into the rougher Rockmead Road. This swings left and drops down to arrive at a T-junction with Lower Waites Lane. Turn right to follow this lane to a T-junction at its end; don't turn right up the road here, but go straight over and immediately right onto what is a signed footpath with fingers pointing right and left. You head briefly with the path towards the sea, but keeping to the path you soon veer sharp left and climb up onto a gentler clifftop, this being your last cliff climb in Sussex. There now follows a really lovely walk on a clearly defined path in the shade of woodland, with beautiful houses to your left and great views ahead to Pett, Winchelsea Beach and, further ahead, towards Camber Sands and the towers of Dungeness. Keeping a magnificent thatched mock-Tudor house to your right, you drop down gently to arrive at a T-junction with a drive, turning left to immediately reach a T-junction with a road. You've now arrived at the village of Cliff End. Turn right to follow the road, soon passing a toilet block and a telephone kiosk; shortly beyond the toilets the road bends sharp left, and as it does so, bear right onto a signed path. This looks distinctly private, but very soon you're reassured by another path sign pointing left. Follow this signed path which shortly takes you to a concrete promenade; looking to your right you can see the promenade ending

Looking towards Cliff End and its sands from the most easterly cliffs in Sussex

and stark cliff faces rising up behind, but you need to turn left to follow the promenade, soon passing the Smuggler Inn and a useful café immediately adjacent to the promenade. Shortly the promenade gives way to an embankment path.

Continue along the embankment path which will take you all the way to Winchelsea Beach. It's an excellent clear path, and a good opportunity to make up for the extra time needed with those tough climbs between Hastings and Firehills! At low tide it's possible to see the roots and stumps of the remnants of a forest inhabited by Stone Age people, but whatever the state of the tide you can enjoy views to the left firstly to the Royal Military Canal and then across Pett Level.

Pett Level and Royal Military Canal

Pett Level is a wide flat expanse of reclaimed land consisting of marshland stretching to the sea and criss-crossed by drainage ditches and canals; it widens out into the immense Romney Marsh, east of Rye. Pett Level is overlooked by the hilltop village of Pett itself, a little way inland and not worth a detour. The beach adjoining Pett Level, stretching north-eastwards towards Winchelsea Beach, is not without interest. At low tide it is possible to see the roots and stumps of the remnants of a forest inhabited by Stone Age people; the trees are about seven thousand years old. To your left, as you set off from Cliff End, you will see the Royal Military Canal which runs parallel with the coastline briefly before turning inland. The canal was built in 1806 and runs all the way to Hythe in Kent. A road was built behind it, the Royal Military Road, to allow fast transport of troops and equipment.

Continue on the embankment path, enjoying views across Pett Level; the disused windmill at Hog's Hill just south-east of the village of Icklesham forms an impressive landmark. As you make progress there are lovely views to the hilltop town of Winchelsea (see below), while to your right is the sea. The sands, even at low tide, are somewhat soggy and uninviting. Roughly two miles beyond cliff End, you pass the straggling and nondescript community of Winchelsea Beach. Access to the village can be obtained by dropping down to Pett Level Road, which runs immediately parallel with the embankment path, and following Pett Level Road north-eastwards away from the sea. By carrying on past the village along Sea Road, the continuation of Pett Level Road, and following this road for another mile, you reach the very beautiful little town of Winchelsea.

Winchelsea

The old town of Winchelsea stood at shore level on a shingle spit on the seaward side where the town is today. By the time of the death of Henry 11 in 1189 it, together with Rye, had become one of the Cinque Ports and by 1229 was supplying ten ships for the English fleet. However, a storm in 1287 washed most of the old town of Winchelsea away. A new town was built on the hilltop, work having in fact started before the storm; it was, on the orders of Edward I, laid out by the Warden of the Cinque Ports and the Lord Mayor of London, the intention being to assist the wine trade with France. The **grid street pattern** of the medieval new town - effectively it is England's first piece of town planning - can still be seen today. Wharves were built on the banks of the river Brede below the town to facilitate its development as a port. The vagaries of nature meant that the town became effectively cut off from the sea, its port had ceased to function by the 15th century, and many of the houses that had been built fell into ruin.

Despite the fact that the town was developed only to a fraction of the size envisaged by Edward I, Winchelsea has many fine buildings. Of particular historical interest are the medieval vaults, which probably served as cellars for the barrels of wine imported from Gascony, and some of which are at least 700 years old. Arguably Winchelsea's chief attraction is the **Church of St Thomas;** although the tower, aisles and nave fell victim to the French, there remains some superb work in the church including canopied and pinnacled tombs dating back to the early 14th century, with Sussex marble effigies. There is a tree in the churchyard called **Wesley's Tree,** so called because it is the descendant of the tree under which John Wesley preached his last open-air sermon in 1790. The other outstanding example of a building which is thought to date from the first days of the town is the **Court Hall,** which contains a museum. Most of the other surviving old buildings of Winchelsea do not date back anything like that far, although in Castle Street is the 14th century house called the

Armoury, and in the garden of Greyfriars in Friars Road stands the ruin of a **Franciscan church** that was built between 1310 and 1320. The original street layout remains, but gracing the streets now are well spaced-out houses, some white-painted, some tile-hung, many decorated with climbing roses and wisteria. Among the prettiest are the 18th century **New Inn** in German Street and the 19th century **Well House** in Castle Street. Winchelsea does have three medieval town gates, namely the early 14th century **Strand Gate,** the early 15th century **Pipewell Gate,** and the medieval **New Gate.** The steep road passing through Strand Gate was described in 1586 as "not strait lest its great declivity should make people tumble headlong as they walk down, or oblige them to go rather on all fours!"

Beyond Winchelsea Beach, where there's a brief promenade, the embankment path ends and you have a choice between veering left to join a metalled coast road or sticking to the beach. The coast road is set well back from the beach and for long stretches you can't see the sea from it, so the beach is the better option. Assuming you opt for the beach, you may then stick to the shingle bank or, depending on the state of the tide, go down onto the sands. The shingle bank is tough going for the most part, although there are some firmer sections, but you do get the best views which include Rye to your half-left and Camber Sands, Camber and Dungeness ahead. The sands, however, provide excellent fast walking, only interrupted by the wooden breakwaters which can be a little tricky to negotiate especially with a bulky pack. That said, there are long stretches which are breakwater-free and the views ahead from the seashore to Camber Sands, Camber and Dungeness are excellent. You're now hastening towards your final river obstruction and inland detour, the mouth of the Rother; if you've opted for the sands you'll be forced back up onto the shingle bank which veers round the landward side of some sea defence works, going forward towards the bank of the Rother estuary. Having arrived at the bank, you can turn left to join a metalled road which will take you to Rye Harbour, the coast road coming up to meet you.

It's very pleasant walking along the metalled track beside the Rother, with good views across to Camber Sands and the end of the walk, a tantalisingly short distance away! In due course you're able to join an embankment path to the right of the metalled road. As you approach the houses of Rye Harbour, look out for an impressively sited Martello tower to your left; at this point, the road and path become separated. Stick to the path which veers round to the right, heading for the Rother, until you get level with Harbour Road heading north-westwards in a straight line towards Rye, and here you descend a short steep slope off the embankment path to join Harbour Road. However if you wished you could, on arriving at the road, bear right and walk the short distance to the William the Conqueror pub and a nicely placed seat with views to the Rother; you could then veer left and wander along the riverside along a path which is actually the course of the old Rye-Rye Harbour freight railway. However there's no way forward, your way blocked by industrial works, so return past the pub to the bottom of Harbour Road.

Rye Harbour and its Nature Reserve

Rye Harbour itself is a pleasant but unremarkable little village with its Martello Tower alluded to above, and its cluster of old fishermen's cottages. Its most interesting feature architecturally is the **Church of the Holy Spirit,** built in Gothic style in 1848-49 and containing fine woodwork in its ceiling, whilst on the wall is a list of those lives saved by the local lifeboat. The village grew as a result of its important strategic position close to the mouth of the river Rother, although the retreat of the sea from the old hilltop town of Rye meant that the old town ceased to function effectively as a port. However, in the mid 19th century, the fortunes of Rye Harbour took a turn for the better: in 1845 a contract for a massive development at Dover Harbour was secured by a firm at Rye Harbour called Lee & Sons, and they collaborated with the harbour commissioners in keeping the entrance clear, using their own dredger. The harbour benefited substantially as a result, and shipyards sprang up. Unfortunately, the fates conspired against the harbour yet again in December 1882 when following a bad storm the harbour entrance was practically blocked. By the First World War Rye Harbour had all but ceased to function as a port, although in later years the fortunes of Rye Harbour did improve with the building by J Alsford Ltd, a timber firm, of a wharf and warehouses.

The nature reserve, beside which you pass as you march from beyond Winchelsea Beach to Rye Harbour, is a birdwatcher's paradise. The 1800 acres of tidal saltmarsh, creeks, river bank and large expanse of shingle, built up by the action of the sea, has

A sundrenched Martello tower at Rye Harbour

been designated a site of Special Scientific Interest. It is on a major migration route and is an important wintering place for seabirds, with many species of wildfowl and waders gathering there to feed in winter. The reserve has not only been important for its scientific interest but also strategically; among defensive constructions to be found here are World War 2 pillboxes and, on the west side of the reserve, **Camber Castle.** This fortress was commissioned by Henry VIII in 1540 but was abandoned in 1643 because of the encroachment of the marshland.

Follow Harbour Road through Rye Harbour village, and having done so you now, in the absence of a riverside path, stay on the same road all the way to its junction with the A259 on the edge of Rye itself. This used to be an absolutely ghastly walk but is now infinitely improved as a result of a cycle/walkway beside the road, which peters out only just at the end. The surroundings are certainly uninspiring at first, with industrial units on each side, but the further you go, you can enjoy increasingly fine views to Rye and also, as you progress, the river Brede, a tributary of the Rother, with its many boats. The road swings to the left to follow beside the Brede - you lose the pavement here, so take care - then swings sharp right to cross the Brede and arrive at the A259. Turn right to follow it into Rye - thankfully there is a pavement available - and cross another river, the Tillingham, then turn immediately right with the A259. Cross the road and continue very briefly beside the A259 riverside road past the Heritage Centre then almost immediately turn left and go forward up the cobbled Mermaid Street. At the top, turn left into West Street, going downhill to meet the High Street in the very centre of Rye.

Rye

It is hard to believe that during the Middle Ages this hilltop town, once a hill fort, was almost ringed by the waters; it stood on a promontory and was linked to the mainland by an easily defensible neck of land, guarded by the estuaries of the Rother and Tillingham. It served as an important port, exporting a number of products to the Continent, including wool and iron, and also old shoes which the affluent folk were prepared to donate to the poverty-stricken French. In the mid-14th century it became one of the Cinque Ports, providing ships for the English fleet, but its defensive importance came at a cost, attracting the attention of French raiders who burned the town in 1377 and again in 1448. Its fortunes as a port suffered severe decline from the 16th century as a result of silting, which left the town 2 miles inland.

Though Rye is still a busy workaday little town, tourism has become more and more important to its well-being, with thousands coming each year to enjoy its charms. The streets of the town, many of them cobbled and narrow, are crammed with historic houses, many weather-boarded, tile-hung or timber-framed, and beautifully preserved. The focal point of the town is **St Mary's Church** which has a remarkable clock, said to have the oldest functioning pendulum in England, dating back to the 16th century. Perhaps the most curious features of the church are the gilded cherubs who strike the bells of the tower clock, although these are modern replicas, the far older originals being kept in the church. Other works of particular interest in Rye are the 14th century **Landgate,** the last remaining of Rye's original three fortified gates; the 13th century **Ypres Tower,** once a prison and latterly a museum; and the **Mermaid Inn,** to be found in the beautiful cobbled Mermaid Street, and containing 13th century features. The High Street boasts the **Old Grammar School,** dating back to 1636, with its distinctive Dutch gables; in Market Street can be found the 15th century timber framed **Flushing Inn** and the 18th century arcaded **Town Hall,** from the balcony of which it has been the custom for the newly-elected Mayor to throw hot pennies to the children below; in Lion Street one will find the 3-storeyed 15th century timber-framed **Fletcher's House;** visitors to Conduit Street will see the remains of the **Augustine Friary,** dating back to 1380; in East Street is the fine Georgian brick-built **Old Vicarage Hotel;** and in West Street is the magnificent 18th century **Lamb House,** where the author Henry James lived, and later another writer E.F. Benson, who wrote the popular *Mapp and Lucia* books.

It should not however be thought that Rye is, or ever has been, a museum piece, shielded from social unrest or disturbance. Smuggling was rife in the town during the 18th and early 19th centuries. One group of smugglers was known as the Hawkhurst Gang, who became notorious among local inhabitants for sitting drinking at the Mermaid Inn with pistols cocked on the table in front of them. There was another equally alarming gang known as the Bonfire Boys, who operated in Rye during the 19th century; they would create effigies of public figures they considered unpopular with them and then burn them.

Nowadays Rye is a much more peaceful place and a lovely town to visit. One of its joys is the profusion of independent shops and absence of big chain stores; one example of a longstanding independent business in Rye is the Martello Bookshop, a deliciously old-fashioned bookshop in the High Street with excellent displays of works by authors associated with the town.

The lovely view of Rye from across the Rother

To leave Rye, continue along the High Street to the point where the houses stop on the right and you reach a little viewpoint with a telescope as the road begins to swing left and drop downhill. Just past the telescope look out for and descend a steep flight of steps to the A259 bypass. Turn left to walk beside the A259 briefly, then cross over using the pedestrian crossing; continue briefly beside the A259 on the far side then very shortly turn right to follow a footpath, passing a toilet block and arriving at a large area of green. Follow this diagonally to its top left corner, aiming for the bridge over the Rother. Cross over the bridge using the right-hand pavement, then immediately beyond the crossing bear right and straightaway right again to join the embankment path beside the Rother heading seawards. Before pressing ahead, pause to enjoy what is a really lovely view of Rye, dominated by the hilltop church.

The embankment path provides really excellent walking and a very much more enjoyable experience than your journey upstream from Rye Harbour to Rye. Assuming you've stopped for refreshment in Rye, and you would have to be very strong-minded not to, you will have a spring in your step! Follow the path, your fast progress interrupted only by a couple of gates/stiles, enjoying excellent views across the river towards Rye Harbour; you're getting the views to the Rother that were denied you on your way up. You pass a lake which is to your left, then beyond the lake your path swings left, away from the Rother, reaching a junction with a track onto which you turn right. You're now on the course of the old railway known as the Rye & Camber Tramway.

The Camber Tramway

The Camber Tramway was the second line of the shoestring railway entrepreneur Colonel Stephens, who was also responsible for the Selsey Tram (see Section 3 above). It opened in 1895 with just one locomotive and one carriage, but later two more locomotives were added, one being petrol powered. The tramway also acquired a second carriage and a small fleet of goods wagons for the transport of shingle from the nearby beach for ballast. Initially the line ran from Rye to the golf links, but an extension to

Straight and true - the splendid green embankment path heading for the sea beside the Rother

Camber Sands was opened in 1908. The line was particularly popular with golfers and also holidaymakers travelling to enjoy Camber Sands (see below). On the outbreak of war, supply dumps were created in the Rye area, and in order to give easy access by military lorries to and from the dumps, areas of the track were concreted over. When the war ended, the cost of re-laying the track proved to be too great, and the line closed for good. Like the Selsey Tram, the Camber Tramway has its fair share of stories: it is said, for instance, that golfing passengers had the habit of pulling out the pin between the first two carriages, leaving the passengers in the second carriage high and dry!

Keep on the track, which skirts Rye golf course, one of the finest links courses in southern England. Although most of the course is to your left, you should watch carefully for golfers driving from the 12th tee situated to the right of the track. It wouldn't do to be knocked unconscious by a golf ball so near to journey's end! Go forward to a gate, and remain on the track briefly beyond it, passing the Harbour Master building which is to your right. Immediately beyond the Harbour Master building, leave the track by turning right and cutting across to rejoin the bank of the Rother. It's now a straightforward and enjoyable walk down to the mouth of the Rother, and satisfying to look back across the river to where you left the seashore some miles back. On reaching the mouth of the Rother, strike out onto Camber Sands and veer left to follow them.

Camber Sands

Camber Sands form one of the best and most popular stretches of beach on your entire walk and indeed on the whole coastline of England; they make a splendid finale to your journey. The superb expanse of gently-ridged golden sand, which stretches out to sea for half a mile or more at low tide, is complemented by extensive sand dunes along the back of the beach. Among the dunes, marram grass has been planted by the Forestry Commission in order to preserve the special qualities of the sands from the effects of the wind.

Continue to enjoy your walk along the sand, choosing your path carefully. The dry sand further back from the mean high tide point makes for marginally faster walking than the wetter sand which can be rather soft and if you choose to walk on it you'll find your boots sinking rather further than you'd wish! On half-decent summer days especially at weekends you may find yourself in the company of swimmers and sunbathers, as this is an extremely popular section of sand. In due course you pass a succession of buildings which signify that you're now level with the buildings of Camber. Just before the point where the buildings end, you'll find that when the tide is high you'll have no sand to walk on and shingle takes over. Don't despair, for it's possible to trudge up the shingle bank to join a concrete promenade which starts immediately beyond the last building. In fact whatever the state of the tide, I recommend you stick to the promenade from which there are excellent views forward to Romney Marsh, the Lydd Ranges, and Dungeness. Immediately below you to your left is the Camber-Lydd road.

Romney Marsh

The area known today as Romney Marsh was originally a saltmarsh but was reclaimed from the sea long ago and is now a mixture of arable land and grazing pasture, home to the white-faced Romney Marsh sheep; the area is exceedingly rich in bird life, and you should look out for wintering lapwings, golden plovers, Bewick's swans, lapwings, migrant fieldfares and redwings, swallows, wagtails and nightingales. To read more about Dungeness, please see my guide to walking the Kent coast (Walking The Kent Coast From End To End, also published by SB Publications).

The promenade peters out and you're faced with a stretch of shingle walking, an annoying imposition so near the end; if you can't face it and the tide precludes your returning to the sands, you could drop down to the car parking area which is to your left and provides firmer walking! The good news is that a further concrete promenade begins a little further along the shore. Enjoying views to the sea - the sands hereabouts are known as Broomhill Sands but at high tide these will be covered - simply plough on along the promenade. You may now hear the sound of gunfire ahead which signals how near you are to Lydd Ranges, a very active military firing range. You pass the untidy assembly of buildings known as Jury's Gap where the Camber-Lydd road turns abruptly inland, and go forward to round a barrier and arrive at a

This far and no further -you cannot continue further along the Sussex coast from this point when firing is taking place on the nearby Lydd Ranges and your coast walk must end here! If you've planned carefully or you've struck lucky you can trudge onwards to the Kent border just half a mile further on

formidable looking gate and fence. You are still half a mile shy of the border with Kent, but if red flags are flying here you cannot go further. Don't try and sneak round the side of the fence; not only will you be liable to challenge for trespassing on MoD property but you may be putting your life at risk. You have no choice but to turn back. Bearing in mind that the final half mile offers no essential change to the surroundings - just more tramping along or behind the beach with Lydd Ranges, Romney Marsh and Dungeness in view - you may feel that this is in any event a good place to call it a day. If you are a purist, though, and want to say you've walked the whole of the Sussex coastline, the enforced curtailment of your walk will undoubtedly be a big disappointment. The answer of course, as I have stated at the start of this section, will be to plan ahead to avoid firing days.

Jeake's House on cobbled Mermaid Street, Rye, sometime home of writer Conrad Aiken, one of many authors who have lived in the town

If you have indeed planned ahead carefully, or if you are simply lucky, and no firing is in progress, you can proceed. I suggest you initially stick to the track beyond the gate; from the track you get a good view of the Lydd Ranges and the countryside beyond it, as well as the sea. Before long, however, the shingle bank may become too tall for you to see the sea properly, so you may wish to make your way down to the shore, albeit the going will be rather tougher on the shingle. As indicated above, you will reach the border with Kent roughly half a mile beyond the gate but there will be no sign that you have completed your walk along the coast of Sussex so without the aid of a GPS device (the approximate grid reference for the border is TR018178) it will be impossible to ascertain the point at which you've reached it. You could put the matter beyond doubt and simply carry on all the way to Dungeness, the towers of which will have been in your sights for much of your walk from Cliff End! Be aware that is a 5 mile walk from Jury's Gap. From Dungeness you could pick up a train on the Romney Hythe & Dymchurch Railway up to New Romney from which there are buses back to Lydd for Rye. However again you will need to have done your homework and checked the railway is running; if it isn't you may need to forge on to Lydd-on-Sea or even to New Romney via Littlestone to find a bus.

Assuming you're at the MoD gate and now (whether you've made it to the border with Kent or not) seeking to turn back towards Jury's Gap and Camber, one last logistical challenge

117

*Arguably Rye's most famous building -
the Mermaid Inn*

awaits you, namely getting back to civilisation. Jury's Gap is on the Lydd-Rye-Hastings bus route but there's no signed bus stop there and it isn't an advertised stop on the official timetable at the time of writing. You can either hope that the driver will stop for you anyway (I suggest you stand at the layby on the bend at the point where the Camber-Lydd road swings inland, and signal to the driver) but if you're not willing to put that to the test, you will have a one-mile trudge back to Camber which will indeed be an anti-climax after reaching journey's end. At least there is a shop and pub in the village, but you may wish to wait till you get back to Rye, with its rail connections, to properly celebrate your achievement in one of its many cafes, teashops, pubs and restaurants. You can there look back on a walk of extraordinary variety and interest, and so many contrasts from clifftop to shingle, from harbour and estuary to grand promenades, from picture postcard villages to bustling ports. Emsworth will certainly seem a very long way back. Congratulations - you have walked the coastline of Sussex!

*One of Rye's many tearooms where you can enjoy a
meal or drink to celebrate the completion of your walk!*

BIBLIOGRAPHY

Sussex - David J Allen - Shire County Guides 1995

The Selsey Tram - David Bathurst - Phillimore 1992

Off The Beaten Track In Sussex - Arthur Stanley Cooke - Herbert Jenkins(nd)

The Illustrated Guide To Britain - Drive Publications 1977

Sussex Place Names - Judith Glover - Countryside Books 1997

The Hutchinson Encyclopedia of Britain - Helicon 1999

Sussex - Arthur Mee - Hodder & Stoughton 1937

Sussex - Esther Meynell - Robert Hale 1947

Sussex (The Buildings of England series) - Ian Nairn and Nikolaus Pevsner - Penguin Books 1965

Philip's County Guides (East and West Sussex) - Philip 1993

The West Sussex Village Book - Tony Wales - Countryside Books 1984

S.B. Publications publish a wide range of local interest books on Sussex.
For a free catalogue please write to:
S.B. Publications, 14 Bishopstone Road, Seaford, East Sussex BN25 2UB
or access our website on
www.sbpublications.co.uk